Proximity to
HISTORY

The Walter Douglas Smith Story

WALT SMITH

PAGE PUBLISHING
Conneaut Lake, PA

First originally published by Page Publishing 2022

ISBN 978-1-6624-7928-1 (pbk)
ISBN 978-1-6624-7929-8 (digital)

Printed in the United States of America

CONTENTS

PROLOGUE

I left the Florence County Probate Court yesterday realizing that I might not ever return to my hometown. I have no reason to return, except to visit the grave site my parents share at the Florence National Cemetery. Snapping in the breeze, American flags towered over the straight ranks of markers in recognition of Veterans Day, reminding me of *Flanders Field*. I have visited the cemetery a handful of times since we lost Dad in his one hundredth year, so I returned for what I thought might be the last time. With no real agenda for after my Probate Court appointment, I drove out to the college. That is how I know Francis Marion University. Taking pictures of the statue erected behind Stokes Hall, honoring him as the founding president, and visiting the Walter Douglas Smith University Center, I stopped for more pictures with my cell phone.

I have always understood the history of the twentieth century within the context of my parent's lives. Dad living past the age of ninety-nine had seen a lot of it. It explains him. Born into the 1918 Spanish influenza, he lost two sisters the year he was born. He was a child of the Great Depression. In 1933, he was fifteen years old. Dad was the face of Tom Brokaw's *Greatest Generation*. His life in that century shaped the sense of duty to family, country, and community that defined him throughout his long life.

On November 22, 2004, when he scribbled his signature, the date and the title to the first page of his memoir, he probably felt he was living on borrowed time at the of age eighty-six. Mom had died from complications of Alzheimer's four years earlier. He had attended the funerals of many of his friends, whose names you will read. When he looked around, much of what he saw in Florence was the change that he had been instrumental in bringing about; but for the story of his life to be more complete, he could have waited another fourteen years to complete *My Life*. I don't remember when he gave it to me. After he died, I jumped through it, looking for the story of meeting my mother in Sydney, Australia—a story I told family and friends assembled for his memorial at First Presbyterian Church in Florence on a miserably cold, rain-drenched day in March 2018.

Dad entered the Second World War as an ensign and left the war as a lieutenant (JG) in the US Navy, commanding PT-138 in the South Pacific. As Mom told the story, Australians would take American officers into their homes, hosting them while on leave from the front lines. She described it as a "twenty-eight-day date"—seven days to get to Sydney, fourteen days of leave, and seven days to return to duty. Because transportation was largely left to the service member to arrange, the navy gave them considerable latitude for their two weeks of leave. Every day that he was in Sydney, they were together. On his last day, Mom gave him a picture. Sitting in the snow on Blue Mountain outside of Sydney, with skis and poles splayed, she was laughing at herself. I don't know if I would describe Dad as a romantic, but seventy-three years later, I found myself standing at the pastor's pulpit, delivering my rambling word-salad eulogy. I pulled from my shirt pocket the picture he had carried in his wallet for all those seventy-three years.

As a personal representative of his estate, I reviewed his funeral instructions, which were reviewed by him and rewritten many times over the years since the manuscript for this book was finished. Changes were few. The manuscript was part of his preparation for March 3, 2018. It was important to him that Ian and I, and our children, have copies of *My Life*. We all have it. I made sure of it. I don't know what the others did, but I did not read it then; and after digging out the bit about Mom for the eulogy, I did not read any further. Maybe I realized then that it was written in anticipation of a time when he would not be around to share his life and times. Reading it would be an acknowledgment he was nearer to leaving us every day. Even when he was gone, I still wasn't ready. As I followed his funeral instructions, I also need to honor his wishes that his story be shared. I owe it to my grandchildren, Rhys and Luna, and to their children.

The life story of Walter Douglas Smith spans from November 17, 1918 to March 3, 2018, from Woodrow Wilson to Donald Trump, through the Great Depression, World War II, and through his life in academia at seven colleges. It is this man's journey through history that is told in *My Life*. With probate of the estate finished, it is time for me to read and share his story in his voice.

HARRIMAN

Perhaps there were others more deserving of the honor, but it was former Union General Walter Harriman, a lifelong resident of New Hampshire, for whom the new city of Harriman, Tennessee, was named in 1890. A year earlier, General Clinton B. Fisk, prohibition candidate for president in 1888, *resolved to create an industrial town that should never have a dram shop in it; a town that was to be an object lesson for thrift, sobriety, superior intelligence, and exalted moral character*" (Harriman Record, 8-5-65).

At Big Emory Gap in Roane County, *"the Emory River breaks through Walden's Ridge after a rapid descent from the Cumberland Plateau. While briefly encamped there, General Harriman was reported to have observed that the area was especially ideal for an industrial city"* (Harriman Record, 8-5-65). That rapid descent was real. As a teen, I fished and swam in those currents many times.

A former New York-born minister and plant manager-turned-real-estate developer, Frederick Gates, appears to have been the one who pitched the idea of marrying the moral purpose of the temperance movement to an attractive business opportunity. His audience was wealthy members of the Women's Christian Temperance Union (WCTU) in the north. Although the WCTU seems fossilized in that period, the movement is international and still active. Gates chartered the East Tennessee Land Company with other prohibitionists and was named the second vice president of the company. Early investors included General Clinton B. Fisk and the founder of Quaker Oats, Ferdinand Schumacher.

1

Col. Robert King Byrd came from a prominent and landed Roane County family. Not burdened by the fact that he owned slaves himself, he was a southern unionist and commanded the Union Army's First Tennessee Infantry after first earning his stripes in the Mexican-American War (1846–1848). When he died in his home in 1885, his widow inherited the 10,000-acre plantation that the East Tennessee Land Company purchased from her for $20,000. M. L. Dame of Knoxville, who attended the land auction, expected lots would sell for $5.00 per front foot. However, bidding by developers who came by Pullman car from as far as Boston began at $75.00 per front foot and went up from there. The dream of Frederick Gates became reality on February 26, 1890, when a successful land auction was held on the front porch of the Byrd mansion. It was the year my father was born. Over three days, 574 lots were sold. It was the year Cy Young would make his major league debut with the Cleveland Spiders, and it was the year that the United States Army would kill hundreds of Lakota Indians, men, women, and children in the massacre at Wounded Knee in South Dakota.

In the short span of three years, the country's giddy appetite for speculation collapsed under the weight of the Panic of 1893. Stock prices wilted, five hundred banks miscarried, fifteen thousand businesses closed, and unemployment hit record highs. Numerous farms ceased operations. Having borrowed one million dollars from the Central Trust Company, the East Tennessee Land Company was overextended and folded. The American Temperance College had been quickly established but survived for less than a dozen years. Some of its buildings remain in use today. The financial panic of 1893 was a rude awakening for investors with dreams of quick profits and continued growth. The population growth of Harriman stagnated, and investors around the country lost their money. The vision of *"an industrial town that should never have a dram shop in it, a town that was to be an object lesson for thrift, sobriety, superior intelligence and exalted moral character"* evaporated.

Despite the damage done by the 1893 panic, generally in those twenty-eight years before my birth, the young town experienced rapid growth. The 1890 census counted 716 citizens. By the next census in 1900, the town had seen 380.7 percent growth to 3,442 citizens. After the success of the auction, the East Tennessee Land Company had ambitiously formed three coordinated subsidiaries to attract industry—the East Tennessee Mining Company, the Harriman Coal and Railroad Company, and the Harriman Manufacturing Company, where my father began work at age fourteen, around 1904. He worked there until his retirement in 1957. Locally, it was called the Plow Shop because it manufactured plows and farm implements sold across the South. General Harriman's vision of industry had materialized. The Harriman, into which I was born, continued its temperance leanings, but the rocketing population growth of the town's early years stalled. At the time of the 2010 census, the population of Harriman was 6,350, and it has since declined.

Twenty-eight years after that first auction on the front porch of the Byrd mansion, I was born on November 17, 1918. In the next year, the Eighteenth Amendment would declare the production, transport, and sale of intoxicating liquors illegal, though it did not outlaw the actual consumption of alcohol. Organized crime seized the opportunity for bootlegging and speakeasies. The Amendment gave birth to stock car racing and the engineering of cars designed to outrun law enforcement. By 1932 and the Great Depression, people were ready for a drink; and repeal of the Eighteenth Amendment became part of the platform that got Democratic presidential candidate, Franklin D. Roosevelt, elected. However, Harriman did not have a liquor store until 1992.

The February 26, 1890 auction was followed by another in May of that year when lots on Walnut Hill at the eastern edge of the initial land sale were sold. Within a year, some one hundred homes had been built there. My parents, Walter Blaine Smith and Jeanette Mae Scarbrough, were married in 1910, and they built on Walnut Hill in 1911. All their children would be born in that house, a two-story wooden structure with four bedrooms upstairs and four rooms down. There were front and back porches overlooking the four-acre plot on which our house was situated. The land provided ample space for a garden that fed the family and a pasture for one or two cows. We were never without milk.

When a spot was found on my mother's lung, the tuberculosis scare came to our home. Popularly called "consumption," the disease was highly contagious. Its victims suffered hacking, bloody coughs, and debilitating pain in the lungs and fatigue. The cause was a bacterium discovered in 1882. Public education campaigns were launched to encourage good hygiene and sanitation practices. The disease could be avoided, but there was no antibiotic treatment available until the 1950s. The most common treatment was fresh air and sunshine. The back porch, with windows all around, became the "sleeping porch." At age ten or eleven, I tested positive, prompting Dad to purchase a policy with Woodmen of the World because it offered sanitarium care, in which exposure to fresh air was the most common feature. We can now safely conclude my testing result was a false positive. I was never diagnosed with the disease, and I was healthy enough for the navy to take me seventeen years later.

It is funny to think about it now, but our house was the last on the street, and we referred to anything past our house as "out in the country." Next door lived my aunt, Laura Scarbrough, my dad's older sister, with my uncle Charles, my mother's older brother. With them lived their two children, Harry born in 1908 and Lois in 1911. I never knew my uncle "Charlie." He had been shot and killed while trying to arrest a man. He was thirty-four years old. Two doors down, lived my uncle, Earl Scarbrough; his wife, Lola; and their children, Norma Rae, Ray, Talmadge, and Christine, who was about my age. She had a sharp mind but was confined to a wheelchair due to complications at birth.

Our house was wired for electricity, and I remember light bulbs suspended from the ceiling by wires. It was plumbed for water to run at the kitchen sink, but there was no bathroom and no indoor toilet. An outhouse sat about fifty yards or so from the backdoor. Baths were "administered" to the children in a large washtub on Saturdays. My mother used a washboard to clean clothing, towels, and sheets until about 1925, when we purchased an electric washing machine, but it had no spin cycle. One of my chores was to man a hand-powered upright roller wringer that squeezed out the water, and another child had the job of taking the still wet clothes to the clothesline.

All the Smith siblings were born and raised in this house on
Route 2, Harriman, Tennessee, built by their parents in 1911.
Doug Smith is pictured here with his youngest son, Walt, in a
shot taken by his granddaughter Miller after a family event.

The field across the road belonged to longtime resident W. W.
Wallace. His unmarried son, Bob, was about the age of my parents
and worked the farm with a fine team of mules. In some years, watermelons were grown in that field, and if I appeared at the right time,
I would be rewarded with one. Pinning the sweet fruit to my chest,
I would race back across the street to submerge it in a slow-flowing
spring on our property. Our source of cold water, it was where we
would chill our tea, milk, and those watermelons in the summer.
Sometimes, Wallace and I would dam the creek to create a small pool
of water to splash in. Follow the flow of the creek about a half mile,
and it spilled into the Emory River. Stern admonishments from our
parents were not enough to keep us from swimming in the river with
other local boys.

When I picture my father, he was about my height (five feet
nine inches) with a medium build and a middle that expanded over
time. In his twenties, his hair thinned to the point of baldness, except
for the wreath that circled his head and a comb-over of a few dark
strands. This had unavoidable genetic consequences for my brother

Wallace and me. Throughout my life in Harriman, my father worked in the machine shop at Harriman Manufacturing Company; and for as long as I can remember, he was the foreman of that shop. From age fourteen to age sixty-five, he reported to work each morning at 6:30 a.m. and worked until 5:00 p.m., at least until labor laws reduced the work day to eight hours. As foreman, it was his responsibility to keep the machinery operating throughout the plant. If parts were not available, he made them. His formal education was limited, but I remember him poring through machinist textbooks when he took correspondence courses.

In the early 1920s, Dad peddled his way to and from work on a bicycle. Around 1925, at the age of thirty-five, he bought a new Chevrolet. It was a four-door touring car with running boards, a canvas top, and the sides were open above the doors. It cost him about $525. A three speed-manual transmission took the 171 cubic inch, four cylinder engine through its paces, packing twenty-six horses under the hood. The coordinated skill set needed to work the clutch—the three speed-gear shift, accelerator, and brakes—was not well practiced in 1925 East Tennessee, and the consequences were predictable. His first attempt at backing out of the neighbor's barn, where it was originally kept, ended with the car in a deep ditch. Dad borrowed the mules from our amused neighbor to pull it out. Seven years later, he purchased a 1932 Oldsmobile that he drove for about a decade, after which it sat idly in the garage for several years during wartime rationing. It was his last car purchase. My mother had no interest in driving. Her use of the car ended after one abortive effort at learning to drive, perhaps due to her unforgiving teacher, my father, but perhaps she saw it has a man's undertaking.

The Great Depression in the United States began in the early 1930s, but life was hard for most people long before then. In Harriman, the Depression came early and stayed late. Parents were hard-pressed to make a living and care for the large families they produced. Birth control lacked options. Children usually did much of the work around the house. I was one of nine children born into the Smith family.

Nineteen eighteen, the year I was born, was very difficult for my parents: having lost a two-year-old daughter, Sybil, and their five-year-old daughter, Wilma, just a few months before I would have become their little brother. My parents were left with two children, Oba and Vivian, until I was born on November 17 of that same year. The 1918, influenza pandemic, sometimes referred to as the "Spanish Flu," was caused by an H1N1 virus of avian origin with deadly properties that were not well understood. The number of resulting deaths worldwide is estimated at 50 million, with around 675,000 of those occurring in the United States, though the real number was probably higher. As with consumption, there were no vaccines available to protect against and no antibiotics to treat the associated bacterial infections. Only non-pharmaceutical interventions were available to contain the virus, such as quarantine, good personal hygiene, use of disinfectants, limiting public gatherings, and practices that were applied unevenly.

In the aftermath, stories emerged illustrating the horror of the time. Young men at a Catholic college and seminary in Philadelphia were assigned to slowly walk with a horse drawn cart down the streets, calling out to announce themselves. When someone called back, the seminarians took turns entering the house to carry a body out to the cart. It is believed that soldiers returning from the war in Europe introduced the disease to this country. Those that did not survive to step off the boat had their remains returned in coffins and were distributed to their hometowns by train. An area art student commuted by train to Chattanooga, taking her through the terminal there. She commented that the coffins "were just everywhere."

A gravedigger in Blount County, Tennessee, the next county over, told this story. "One morning, at 6:00 a.m., I was set to work digging three graves for a family of six that lived down the road from my home. Around 9:00 a.m., the doctor sent word to dig yet another grave. Then around lunchtime, I got word to dig yet another grave, and by 4:00 p.m., I was instructed to dig the final grave for that entire family."

The deaths sometimes outpaced coffin availability, and the burials were sometimes referred to as "plantings." Despite what the country was seeing, in San Francisco and other places, hostility to common-sense measures developed on the grounds of personal liberty. It was led by a loose coalition of constitutional conservatives that came to be known as the Anti-Mask League. Predictably, infections spiked.

The influenza epidemic visited death among many area families, and I marvel at the strength of my mother, losing two children and giving birth to a third in the space of one year. The sisters I would never know were interred in a hilltop cemetery not far from the house, and during my eighteen years at home, I would go with Dad to mow the grass on the Smith plot, in my younger years, climbing on the tombstones while my father worked.

Walnut Hill Baptist Church was fundamental to the lives of my parents, who were founding members. For most of his life, Dad was a deacon and a Sunday-school teacher. Even now, I can imagine Dad sitting by a lamp on Saturday night, preparing the next day's lesson. My mother was a faithful and devoted church member, participating in the activities of the church women, reading her Bible regularly, and underlining her favorite passages.

In the Baptist Church, it seemed to be accepted fact that age twelve was the age of accountability; when a child was old enough

to make a declaration of faith and be "saved," and so it was that when I reached the age of twelve, my mother handed me the Bible and declared that it was time for me to "accept Christ." I took the Bible from her but did not know what she meant. I had been to church and revivals all my life and had seen people go to the mourner's bench up front and sit with head down while members of the congregation filed by and said something to them. I knew with certainty that there was a Jesus in heaven, but I did not know what was to happen up front when our time came. When it did, Wallace and I obediently took our places at the mourner's bench and sat with our heads reverently bowed. When nothing happened, we arose from the bench, shook hands with the pastor, and our names were listed among the "saved."

Walnut Hill Baptist Church had its share of "backsliders" at the revivals. They had been there before: people who felt the spirit move them to cry out in paroxysms of joy they felt in the grace of the Father. They might not be seen in church again until the next revival. Whatever my mother's expectations, at age twelve, I was far from understanding what it was all about. However, I suppose regular exposure to the church, the teachings, and the good examples provided by my parents instilled in me internal rules about living a moral and ethical life. Retrospectively, at age twelve, I needed more explanation and evidence and less fear and damnation. The Smith kids all became members of Walnut Hill Baptist Church, but then, we probably did not feel any choice in the matter.

Providing for seven children on a very modest income, my parents were very careful with their resources. Only if something was needed, and we could not make it or grow it was money spent, and with Dad's skills, that didn't leave much. I managed a productive garden each year, growing fresh vegetables during the summer and a good store of potatoes. We canned apples, peaches, beans, and tomatoes for the family's winter consumption. Almost anything can be canned and done properly; food will last four to five years. The process Mom used was to put the food in the jar, usually a Kerr jar, and heating them to a temperature that destroys the microorganisms that cause food to spoil. In the heating process, air is driven from the jar and a vacuum seal is formed. From year to year, we could clean and reuse the jar, but the lids were for one use only. Afterward, the canned food would be kept in a cool place.

At around age twelve, I was assigned to milking the cows, both in the morning and at night. That job also carried responsibility for cleaning out the stable and putting hay or fodder in the manger for the cows. There was always a hog in a pen that required feeding at least twice each day. In the first cold days of November, it was time to slaughter the hog, and neighbor men arrived for the butchering; their efforts rewarded by taking home some of the meat. Ham was the entre at most meals throughout the winter, including my school lunch, and cold ham biscuits, which I still enjoy.

Our lives had not changed much from the nineteenth century. We grew corn and hauled it to the local gristmill for grinding into meal for cornbread. As the oldest son, hauling the corn and bringing home the meal, as well as many other jobs, fell to me. I marveled at the contraption the old gentleman used for the job. Sometimes, powered by a stream of water turning a wheel, his was a steam-powered road-roller's flywheel attached to a long belt that turned the millstone.

By today's standards, we might have been labeled "poor," but my father never missed a paycheck in his life; we were fed and clothed; our food from the garden was fresh or stored in jars in the basement. We had very few toys, and at Christmas, one or two gifts were all we expected or received. There were a couple of years that only clothes were under the tree, but our expectations were not high, so the disappointment did not last long. I remember getting a wagon when I was quite young. Successively, it was also enjoyed by the younger siblings that followed me. I bought a used bicycle when I was about fifteen, fixed it up, and used it for several years. In or around 1932, Dad accompanied a group of men to the Chicago World's Fair, returning with small gyroscopes for each of his sons. To us, they were magical.

As I write this at the age of eighty-three, I might be forgiven for not recalling childhood events with crystal clarity. But, among my earliest memories, was a black walnut tree outside of our backdoor. As with all the food we grew, it was also subject to harvesting. After collecting a basket full, my oldest sister Oba would bring me inside to remove the nuts from the hulls. A new crop of walnuts that were not completely dry would stain my hands black. As well, I have the vague memory of being a five-year-old, and perhaps it was on this birthday that my uncle Doug (Scarbrough), for whom I am named, gave me a twenty-dollar gold coin. My mother took custody of it until I was grown, and perhaps, she should have held on to it since I cannot account for it today.

There were times in my early years when we were told that Mom was "sick." Aunt Laura and other women in the family would sit with her for the day. My siblings and I were ordered out of the house or to stay quiet. Some of those days stretched into the night. When the "sickness" was over, the children were invited in to meet a new baby brother or sister. This happened four times for me, bringing the number of children in the family to seven. There were also times when our household of nine was brought to ten. I have many memories of Grandpa Scarbrough (1856–1947), who lived with us from time to time, and Aunt Callie Scarbrough, my mother's youngest sister, who lived with us for six to eight years.

It was two months before my sixth birthday in 1924 that schooling began for me. With my sisters, Oba and Vivian, I walked the mile from our Walnut Hill home to the combined elementary and high school, the same site on N. Roane Street as the high school that stands there today. On cold and rainy days, the walk was miserable and seemed longer. It was not the ten-mile hike through snowdrifts uphill in both directions I would later describe to my children, but it was miserable. There were no kindergartens in town, leaving parents on their own to prepare their children for school. Some were better prepared than others. My parents were intelligent but had little formal education themselves, handicapping my own preparation for school, though they strongly supported school and enforced study time. My father's schooling ended after four years, and Mom managed six years. At the time, long years of education were not considered important for kids who would be working on farms and in factories. When I arrived at school, skinny and immature, I was corralled into a classroom filled with children who had never been exposed to the discipline of a classroom, with teachers whose training might have been limited to a year or so of college. At the conclusion of that first year of school, I was promoted to "high first grade," a spin on saying I was being held back.

Life and schooling improved in 1925. The city schools were crowded, and a short-term decision was made. Walnut Hill Baptist

Church would host school for area children in first through fourth grade while a new Walnut Hill Elementary School was being built only a little more than a quarter mile from our house. In a large Sunday-school room, Mrs. Jarvis, wife of the city school superintendent, presided over the four grades. I was able to listen to the third- and fourth-grade students reciting their lessons as I learned my own. There, I became a legitimate second grader.

Before long, Mrs. Jarvis was shepherding her students into a stucco cinder-block building, housing two classrooms for four grades. I could not now say whether she was a good teacher, but I do remember being rewarded for completing our assignments with readings from classic literature, *Beowulf*, Robin Hood, *Ulysses*, Achilles, and other children's books, in a classroom circled with alphabet cards and blackboards on the wall.

Each fall, before the start of school, the family would pile into the Oldsmobile, and Dad would drive the ten miles to the JC Penny store in Rockwood, one of 674 across the country at the time. It was time to purchase new clothes and shoes for the coming semester. I was fascinated by the vacuum tubes used to facilitate our purchase, like those seen at the bank drive-through today. The store clerk would place orders and money into a canister, and it raced through a clear tube to the business office on the second floor, racing back to the salesman with the receipt. By today's standards, we were not well-clothed, but we had it better than most. No one had much, particularly during the long Depression years.

Generally, I did not wear shoes from May until school started, not even to church on Sunday, but school was another matter. Our shoes were not very good but had to make it through the school year. A "shoe last" is a mechanical form, shaped like a human foot, used in the manufacture and repair of shoes, and that is how Dad got us through the school year. However, neither the original soles, nor Dad's replacements, were effective in keeping water out. On rainy days, I left the house for school knowing I would have wet feet by the time I got there.

As a child, I was skinny with red hair and freckles, and I trailed my friends on the growth chart. Brushing my teeth was encouraged, but no one was checking to see if my toothbrush was wet. There was no lack of exercise. Children were put to work early in those days, and when I was about seven or eight, I joined my parents and Grandpa at tending to the family garden. Wallace was not far behind. The girls were assigned to indoor chores. This continued until high-school graduation and my departure for McDonald, Ohio, where my adult life would begin.

As I advanced through grade school, my work continued to improve. I say this with the memory of my transition from fourth grade at Walnut Hill Elementary School to fifth grade at the main school in town. Still, there were too many students, there was too little space, and too few teachers; so again, overcrowding forced a decision. Based on my progress, I was suddenly a sixth grader—a skinny, undersized, and terror-stricken sixth grader. Girls towered over me, and the boys who were held back looked like grown men. My unusual transition from fourth to sixth grade earned me no special consideration from the teacher, Miss Denton. I was an academic castaway, lost and on my own. This was reflected in my grades, "*Ms*" and "*Ns*," representing failure or borderline success. I felt then and now that with a little extra attention from Miss Denton, I would have advanced to the seventh grade at the end of the school year, but when the summer ended and the new school year began, I was still in the sixth grade, taught by the same teacher. Twice held back, that experience was never going to be repeated.

There were always several larger boys who had been held back until they were allowed to drop out after the eighth grade, so ninth grade became something of an equalizer. We were all about the same age, and by the time I reached my senior year, I had grown to five-foot-eight-inch tall and weighed 137 pounds, more or less average for my class, but still not large enough for the football coach to notice me. Nevertheless, in 1936, among the smaller boys, I played end on the Harriman High football team. There were only two boys topping 200 pounds, Joe Goddard and "Fats" Claborne. Two years later, Joe was my roommate at Lincoln Memorial University. In a week, he was gone, withdrawing under the influence of being homesick.

The Harriman team usually posted winning records, playing against other small area schools like ours. However, in 1936, Coach George Ballard scheduled a game with Central High of Knoxville, a "farm club" for the head coach at the University of Tennessee, Major Bob Neyland, for whom the stadium there now would be named in 1962. In recruiting for the university, Neyland and his staff would find good high-school players from across the country and arrange for their families to move to Knoxville. The boys would join the Central football team, and their fathers were given jobs by UT boosters. With the economy still mired in the Depression, the offer of a good job was a convincing incentive. Ray Graves of neighboring Rockwood was one of those players who moved to join the Central team, then transitioning to UT. He went on to become the head football coach at the University of Florida. Well, over 200 pounds, Graves played at the left tackle position. At 137 pounds, it became my job to block him and still survive high school. My strategy was not one taught by the coaches. As Graves pushed by me, I struggled to slow him, get in his way, and even to hook his ankles so he had to drag me toward our quarterback and best player, Fred Moore. The results were what you might expect. The Harriman High "Devils" were annihilated by the "Bobcats," 55–6. It is still a matter of pride that we were not blanked. Indicative of the time, before clambering onto the bus for our forty-mile return to Harriman, Coach Ballard doled out thirty cents to each player to purchase a hamburger for dinner, recognizing some of them might not have dinner waiting on them at home.

I did not enjoy football. It was a cultural thing that boys did. I suppose it still is. It brought some recognition and respect from our peers, and some self-respect, none of which compensated for my limping, aching body from September to December. The equipment was poor. The school furnished uniforms worn by several previous generations of players, and we had to provide our own cleats. That cost my parents $8. My time on the team was limited to my senior year. I accepted my letter and bought a sweater on which to sew it. I don't think football did anything to improve my character as some might advocate.

For adolescents, Harriman was beyond dull, providing little in the way of a social life. Wake up, do chores, go to school, come home and do more chores, study, go to bed, wake up, and repeat. The routine was sometimes interrupted by going to basketball games, the occasional school play and, of course, football season. I never dated. In the 1930s, very few of us did. There was no YMCA, but I could jump in the Emory River at a place where the city had leveled the bank and installed two diving boards. There was no scouting troop in the Walnut Hill area, and there was no place for kids to just "hang out." Regarded by my parents as an evil gambling den, there was a poolroom on Roane Street where I played a few games when I was seventeen or eighteen. I saw no evil in it, but I also never told my parents. Churches helped a bit, but not significantly. There were no outreach programs for young people as there are now. I was in Christmas plays at church when I was very young, and in late adolescence, I sang in the choir...on the back row, unseen and unheard. It was a fundamentalist Baptist Church established in a town founded by prohibitionist, which is, to say, had a limited sense of what fun meant to a teenager. I am reluctant to call it a "social activity," but funeral services held some perverse interest for me in early childhood, particularly the congregational procession by the casket to view the remains of the departed member. I studied the faces of the decedents and wondered about the mystery of death.

Even if one had never seen it, one can still imagine the old white wood-framed church building that was probably constructed before the turn of the century. It survived until around 1935, when a new brick building was erected to replace it. Dad set an example for us, contributing his time tithing and labor when needed. I was sixteen and volunteered my labor to the construction. Even today, I carry a reminder of working at the church, a scar above my left eye, courtesy of a shovel wielding Junior Self, who accidentally struck me there. Wounds of that nature were generally treated at home, so I did not see a doctor. Months passed before the wound became a scar.

Dad took his rules for living directly from the Bible. His religion was more cerebral than emotional and less likely to be swayed by church politics, which have always existed. Baptists churches seem more vulnerable to the schisms among members that lead to break-ups, and in the years after I left home, Walnut Hill Baptist succumbed to such a division. It created an awkward moment for my parents. Mom left the church. Dad, of course, sided with my mother philo-sophically but declared that as a founder of the church, he would not be driven out. He remained a member until his own funeral there.

In ours, family ties were very important. I think my mother was Uncle Doug's favorite sister, and as his namesake, he seemed to feel some obligation toward me. When I was fifteen, he and Aunt Nettie made the trip from McDonald, Ohio, to Harriman for a visit, about a 550-mile drive. When they left Harriman, I went with them, seeing countryside that was very different from the familiar East Tennessee landscape. It was 1934, and Doug had a good job with US Steel as a roller in the mills. Uncle Doug and Aunt Nettie, and their chil-dren—Bob, Chuck, Joyce, and Evadean—shared their home with me and took me to a weeklong summer-church retreat at a lake. In three years, I would return to work in the steel mills and see some of the same kids I met at the lake. I am not sure how I got home, but it was possibly by train. It was a route that would later become very familiar.

With graduation from Harriman High School in 1937, I turned the page from my life in that small East Tennessee town, and I looked to the future. Nationally, the economy was slowly emerging from the Depression, but that was hardly noticeable in Harriman. There were no jobs, no scholarships, and no loans available for aspiring college students without ample collateral. I wanted to go to college, and Uncle Doug gave me that opportunity.

MCDONALD

In June of 1937, with my family in attendance, I crossed the stage to receive my high-school diploma. That evening, around 9:00 p.m., Dad drove me the three or four miles to the Harriman Junction. I was heading north to McDonald, where I would join Uncle Doug at a steel mill. Boarding a passenger car, I gave a goodbye wave to Dad and showed the conductor my seven-dollar ticket, leaving me with $10 in my wallet. It was with trepidation, excitement, and anticipation that I set off for my first year in the steel mill, again to live with Uncle Doug and Aunt Nettie. Pulled by a steam locomotive, the track took me through many mountain tunnels in Tennessee and Kentucky. The windows were closed, but that did little to stop the coal smoke from seeping into the passenger car, where the acrid smell would linger in the air. Boarding the train at the Harriman Junction around 9:00 p.m., I would arrive in Niles, Ohio, twenty-one hours later, around 6:00 p.m. As we approached periodic stops, the conductor would call out the names of the towns. People disembarked with their luggage, and people climbed aboard with their luggage. I slept as much as the commotion would allow. Taking the interstate today, the trip could be made in about nine hours. The stop in Cincinnati, where I was to connect with the train to Niles, was about halfway there. On entering the large station, with people constantly coming and going, I made nervous inquiries about my connection to Niles, the departure time, and track. On that first trip, I did not stray from the station; but on a later trip, I ventured out of the station to the movie theater across the street to see one of three "singing cow-boy" movies, starring Tex Ritter, released in 1937. The movie ticket cost me ten cents.

I boarded the train for Niles around midday. We meandered our way north and east through Ohio, and I can still hear the conductor as he broadcasted the names of the towns and cities where still more passengers departed and others would board—Columbus, Newark, Canton, and finally in the early evening, Niles. I called Uncle Doug's house and found cousin Bob ready to bring me the two or three miles to McDonald. The house was full, with two people in every bed. It is an unusual practice today, but not in 1937.

I never would have gotten the steel-mill job without my uncle's influence, and I would not have found a job in Harriman that paid as well. The country was still recovering from a devastated economy, and jobs were hard to find. Designated the no. 17 mill, I worked at the Carnegie-Illinois subsidiary of US Steel, the newest at the McDonald plant. Most of the eight or so rolling mills there dated back to 1918. The no. 17 plant had been in operation for about ten years at that time. Compared to the mills of today, they were dinosaurs.

We produced a variety of sheet steel in sizes from a few inches in width, a thickness of up to a quarter of an inch, and in lengths from four feet to perhaps twenty feet. Long sheets of steel emerging from the rollers would be cut to the specifications of the purchaser and were then "pickled" in an immersion of hot acid solution for about ten minutes, then in a neutralizing base solution. Working in pairs, one man on each side of the sheets, they were lifted on to a long wagon with comblike slots into which the sheets were placed. My weight and strength had not changed in the few months since Ray Graves ran over me, and my first summer week of wrangling sheets of steel in a hot steel mill was hell! My partner, a man of about thirty-five years of age, was intolerant toward my lack of experience, but I persevered; and after a few weeks, I began to catch on to prac-tices that made the job easier, like knowing when and how to convert the horizontal sliding movement of the sheet into a vertical lift that expertly placed it into the slots of the comb. I was also getting stron-ger with each eight-hour day. At age eighteen, putting on muscle comes easy. I would leave my shift at the mill dripping in sweat and physically whipped. By the time I left McDonald in August of 1938, I weighed eighteen pounds more than when I had arrived, and it was all muscle. Every shift was eight hours of weight lifting. Shifts at the mill ran from 8:00 a.m. to 4:00 p.m., one week; 4:00 p.m. to midnight, the next; and midnight to 8:00 a.m. the next; and my body was constantly adjusting. I was paid $1 per hour. For my room and board, I gave Aunt Nettie $15 per month and sent the balance home to my mother for deposit to my bank account. By the end of my first year in the steel mill, I had saved about $1,000.

My social life in McDonald did not improve from Harriman. I was single-minded about saving for college. I was not distracted by every boy's goal of buying a car, and my social life suffered for lack of transportation. Some three miles from the Scarbrough house, there was a movie theater in Gerard, where I could take in a film, not often with a girl. The YMCA and a drug store soda fountain were the hangouts for young men in the small mill town. Sunday mornings were spent at church with Doug's family, though Chuck was not often with us, coming in late on Saturday nights and sleeping late on Sunday mornings. In his late twenties, his parents tolerated his absence, and I suspect Uncle Doug's exposure to all sorts of people at the mill contributed to his tolerance.

Uncle Doug was a roller, in charge of the actual production lines. Education separated rollers from superintendents. Rollers were the old-timers, coming through the ranks. Superintendents were likely to be college graduates who were better equipped for paperwork and personnel issues, people like cousin Bob, who graduated from Westminster College (Pennsylvania), where he was the fullback on the football team. He was in management.

I remained in McDonald working in the mill until August 1939. Often, there were insufficient orders for steel, and the mill operations would be down to a couple of days a week. Employees would consult a large blackboard on the outside wall of the centrally located firehouse to learn if their mill was operating. There were many weeks when the no. 17 mill operated only a few days a week, slowing my savings. We did not put the Great Depression behind us until 1939 and World War II, when the entire country was put to work.

LINCOLN MEMORIAL
UNIVERSITY

In the summer of 1938, the train rails that had taken me to McDonald on the day I had graduated from high school took me home. I had saved $1,000, and it was time to enroll in college. Dad was amazed at my physical appearance, carrying an extra eighteen pounds of muscle. It was nice to be home, but it was to be only a short visit. On the second day back, I ran into Harry Lafon, a former classmate. He was wearing the uniform of an army second lieutenant and had joined the National Guard. As National Guard units were federalized, Harry's military attachments would change. He was a student at Lincoln Memorial University in Harrogate, Tennessee. I was considering entering the freshman class at the University of Tennessee or Carson Newman. But Harry spoke about LMU in glowing superlatives and added that I could work there to cover much of my college expenses. I suppose now that many schools had similar programs, but Harry was convincing. I wrote to the school with admission inquiries. I was accepted, and without one visit before the first day of classes, I entered as a freshman. By this time, the Oldsmobile was sitting in the garage, unused—a decision perhaps initially driven by Dad's lifetime of thrift. His brother Charlie, who also worked at Harriman Manufacturing Company, stopped at the house each morning to give him a ride to work. It was Uncle Charlie, Dad, and me, with my few possessions in Charlie's car for the 100-mile trip to LMU, located in the Cumberland Gap of the Appalachians. I was to be an LMU "Railsplitter."

I was assigned to a third floor corner room in DAR Hall, where I found Joe Goddard, the 200-pound teammate at Harriman High, who would be gone in a week. A new roommate was not assigned that year. Joe did all right though. A year later, he enrolled in the University of Tennessee and continued through his doctorate, later becoming an administrator in the UT Extension Program.

Harry Lafon was still there until 1942, when he went on active military duty and was shipped out to the Philippines. He was stranded on Bataan and survived the death march, only to later die onboard a prisoner ship bound for Japan that was torpedoed by an American submarine. On August 18, 1944, American intelligence intercepted a message from Japanese command that the Shinyo Maru was being sent to Zamboanga. It was misinterpreted to say the ship was to transport military personnel. That should have read military prisoners. At 7:37 p.m., on September 7, 1944, the USS Paddle spotted a Japanese convoy and put two torpedoes into the ship. Surviving POW witnesses who managed to escape the ship's holds described the massive explosion and how the Shinyo Maru seemed to bend in the middle before sinking into the ocean. Of the 750 prisoners on board, eighty-three were rescued by Filipino guerillas. Harry was not one of them.

Majoring in chemistry, I also enrolled in English, Mathematics, Mechanical Drawing, and History. I enjoyed LMU, though I was not dazzled by my professors, and the library was inadequate. It would fail to meet accreditation standards today. Freshman English taught me nothing that I did not carry away from high school. History class amounted to dull recitations from a textbook. Mathematics classes added little to nothing that Mrs. Alford had taught me in high school. I had no talent for mechanical drawing and no interest in it. Chemistry was not available to me in Harriman, and if for no other reason, the novelty of it made it interesting. Professor Johnson came to LMU with a master's degree and an employment history that included a laboratory in Copperhill, Tennessee, in the hills just north of the line with Georgia. He hired me as his lab assistant. Though my grades were good, I was not inspired and ultimately concluded I had no natural talent for chemistry either.

I was also given a job in the kitchen. Cooking, serving, cleaning, and all other menial tasks attached to kitchen work became my job. It earned me seventeen cents per hour. Working about eighteen hours per week, I could earn about $150 in a year that would be applied against my 400-dollar-per-year tuition. I was on track to spend my college savings in no more than two years.

Life was campus centered. Having no car made sure of it. I worked, studied, and met socially with my classmates. Improving upon my previous social life, I had dates with two or three girls in that first year. Elsie Legarde, a cute girl from Cleveland, Tennessee, comes to mind. She was my first on campus date. A long-term relationship was not meant to be. In fact, it didn't last long enough to merit the term "break up." In my sophomore year, my roommate was Vernon Wallen, and for a few months, I went out with his cousin from Blackwater Virginia, Dolly Wallen. There were others in my first two years at college—Alice Henry, Helen Braden, Jean Thomas, Polly Ford and more—but there were no love affairs; frequently they were only dates for on-campus dances. After dinner each night, guys would stop by Lafrentz Hall, the women's dormitory. The entire basement was a recreation room. A jukebox played the sentimental dance favorites of the late 1930s, Glenn Miller, Count Basie, Duke Ellington, as couples took their turns on the dance floor. None of the girls mentioned will remember me for my dancing, at least not in a good way. A bell sounded at 7:00 p.m., and the men left the building: some extending their time with a girl by going to the library until closing at 9:00 p.m.

The LMU fraternities and sororities were all local organizations. Each had a social room in one of the campus buildings, and each hosted a dance each year for the members and their dates, always chaperoned by faculty couples, who I imagine were both amused and bored. Women tended to be strictly supervised while the rules for men were frequently ignored. I joined Sigma Pi Beta; it's motto, "Onward through the Fog." The motto was later adopted by "Oat Willies," the oldest continuously run head shop in the country located in Austin. As a motto, it seems more appropriate to a head shop than a small college fraternity.

Sigma Pi Beta fraternity at LMU. In the flannel shirt,
Doug Smith is fifth from the left of the back row.

Highway 32 would take you northwest from Harrogate and over a mountain to Middlesboro, Kentucky, with its movie house and shops. Guys generally hitched a ride, though on Sundays, we would board a train from the previous century and ride through the tunnel to Middlesboro. In the passenger car, a potbellied coal stove kept the riders warm in winter.

As my sophomore year ended, so did my savings, and my studies took a break. I called Uncle Doug.

BACK TO MCDONALD

The first year of the 1940s was dominated by war-related news. The Germans had opened Auschwitz, the Battle of Britain raged, and London suffered daily bombing. Roosevelt was in his third term, and I was back in Ohio, working on a railroad track-maintenance crew, with a very large Italian man as foreman. The track was designed for slag cars, hauling ash and waste products from the furnaces in Youngstown. Previously, and for many years, the slag was simply dumped over a large area near the Carnegie-Illinois plant in McDonald. Today, it would be enough to make an environmentalist weep, but it was now being repurposed into building roads. There were acres of the stuff, fifteen to twenty feet deep, and the job was year round.

The crew was a mixed lot and included several Italians. With nothing more than a whistle and a gesture from the foreman, the crew would move on to the next task, his authority unquestioned. As fall turned to winter, the weather turned cold and icy, and I was out in it, though I wasn't suffering for it. My next assignment was to the rock-crushing plant. Slag was pulverized and loaded to waiting trucks through large chutes. There were various jobs for me that year. One was to knock loose the pins holding the slag car doors, allowing the slag to pour down a chute to be crushed. In another job, I controlled the chutes to the trucks carrying away the finished product. The most difficult task was to control the slag cars waiting on an inclined grade to be loaded by a large steam-driven shovel. Inching the car down the grade into position for the shovel operator was complicated by undependable hand brakes on the ancient cars. Locating the car in just the right place was a challenge, and on occasion, a car would get out of control and drift down the grade for a hundred feet. A locomotive would be called to push it back into position. There was no joy in this job, but my performance must have been good since I was kept in it for several weeks.

In a steel mill, a "cobble" is a great tangle of red hot steel that results when fast-moving steel coming through the rollers fails to go through the next set of rapidly revolving rollers. The cobble is then pulled away by a crane. At some point, I was moved into no. 12, where small-sized steel and angle iron were rolled, and for several months, my job was to cut the cobble into smaller pieces with an acetylene torch.

At other points, I was in shipping, loading box cars with finished steel, or on a crew inserting a wire through rolled steel with the objective of twisting the wire snugly and holding together the roll. The steel was hot, probably in excess of one thousand degrees, and we wore asbestos gloves that were not always equal to the job, leaving blisters burned on my hands that were treated in the infirmary. When the superintendent decided I was reasonably intelligent, I was given my best assignment, working outside in the steelyard, finding proper steel bars for the order being rolled and summoning a crane to pick it up. It was then transported by the overhead crane to the furnaces for heating in preparation for the rolling process. Willard Scarbrough was in charge of that furnace and was my mother's first cousin. One weekend, the furnace had been down for a few days, and I had the surreal experience of entering the furnace to clean it.

Outside of the mill, my uneventful life in McDonald was occasionally interrupted with a movie and a date. My cousins had all married and moved away. I say uneventful, but there was the strike. I attended a union meeting in McDonald. Wild and passionate speeches were made, culminating in a vote to strike. I did not belong to the union, and working in a steel mill after college was not part of my vision for the future. Bob was in management, and Uncle Doug was considered management by reason of his tenure. One day, riding to the mill with them, a large group of pickets could be seen in the distance, attempting to keep workers from going into the plant. With the thought that my presence in the car could become problematic for Bob and Uncle Doug, I got out of the car and walked to the gate, going through unnoticed and unmolested. Doug and Bob, however, were stopped and harassed. Later, both teased me about abandoning them.

My second year at the steel mill drew to a close in the summer of 1941, and I returned to Harriman before heading to Harrogate. My brother Wallace married Alma Brewer, fresh out of high school, and sister Vee and Benny Yeary had married as well, so Mom and Dad had fewer plates on the dinner table.

RETURN TO LINCOLN
MEMORIAL UNIVERSITY

I was happy to be back on campus on September of 1941, unaware that in about two months, 353 Japanese bombers would scuttle nineteen US ships, destroy 188 US aircraft, and kill two thousand Americans in Pearl Harbor. The attack would propel the United States into the worldwide conflict and, in many ways, shape my life. It was the moment we learned to number our world wars.

I lived in Grant-Lee Hall, a two-and-a-half-story building constructed on the limestone foundations of a previous building completed in 1892. The luxury Four Seasons Hotel and Sanitarium had hosted many famous guests, including Cornelius "Commodore" Vanderbilt, for whom the University was named, and Mark Twain. On the north side of campus, the naming of the building for civil-war generals on opposite sides of the conflict was intended to commemorate post-civil-war healing from the war in the East Tennessee region. One of my roommates was Gorman Hill, also a junior, who had come to LMU with his twin sister, Jennie. My other roommate was Zeb Presnell, a five foot six sophomore, who I remember as a surprisingly good basketball player.

Life on the campus of a small college has advantages that seem rooted in simplicity. Located near the Cumberland Gap at the converging borders of Tennessee, Kentucky, and Virginia, LMU is surrounded by towering mountains. It is a rural setting. People knew each other. When I was there, the enrollment was about five hundred. Students mostly lived on campus in three residence halls, DAR, and Grant-Lee for the men, and Lafrentz Hall for the women. It was small enough that no student would be unnoticed, and I probably knew every student there by name, including the commuters. Everyone was involved in social activities; however, it was a conservative social life that was stricter for the women than the men. Women were required to register when they left the dorm and when they returned. Alcohol consumption was strictly forbidden, though most of the men would imbibe moderately. There were no "recreational" drugs. This conservative life was at least partially enforced by the lack of money. People were still poor; many students coming from families unable to provide much in the way of support. Few had a car, which simplified parking issues. Ten dollars a month would have exceeded the budget for many, and I was very frugal with my money. The race between graduation and running out of savings first was neck and neck.

I continued my major in chemistry into my junior year, working my eighteen to twenty hours per week as a lab assistant and managing one or two laboratory sections. I suspect that a student coming out of high school today knows more chemistry than I did finishing my senior year at LMU, but I completed my hours as a chemistry major, and after completing my foreign language requirement, I would ultimately graduate with minors in mathematics and physics, with a year of biology, to my credit.

The year 1941 had been a good year for me. I had a girlfriend, my college work was satisfactory, and I was anticipating graduation, followed by a job after another year. That changed on December 7, 1941. With Mary Helen Carter from a nearby town in Virginia and two other couples, I climbed into Tommy Beatty's car, and he drove us into Middlesboro, Kentucky, to see a movie. He returned to the sandwich shop he managed in Harrogate and came back for us when the movie let out, around 5:00 p.m. It was Tommy Beatty who delivered the sobering news to us that the Japanese had attacked Pearl Harbor. The country had been uneasy for months and most expected war, and in that moment, the guys in the car understood they would soon be wearing the uniforms of the United States military.

Until World War II, my birthday was celebrated on November 18, the day insisted upon by my mother. As the story goes, the doctor had been summoned to the house for my imminent arrival on the 17, but I was in no hurry and arrived in the early morning hours of the 18. The State of Tennessee did not issue birth certificates in 1918. Doctors submitted a birth notice to Nashville for recording purposes. At the age of twenty-three in 1942, I applied for a birth certificate for purposes of enlisting in the navy. When the certificate arrived, it stated my birth date as November 17, 1918. The event of my birth is not likely something my mother would get wrong, but a tired and sleepy doctor might not have noticed that a new day was dawning. As a result, I was eligible for social security benefits a day early!

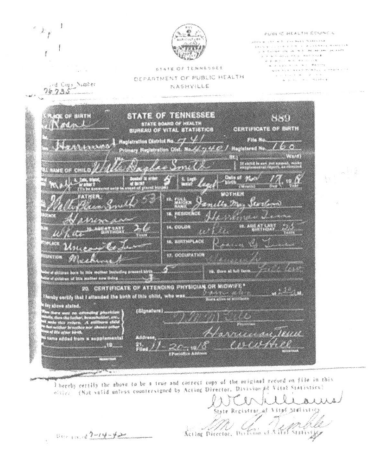

It was sometime after Christmas of 1942 that I went to the recruiting office in Middlesboro, volunteered for the navy, and was given a V-7 enlistment status, meaning that I could complete my senior year of college before beginning active duty as a Midshipman. My choice of military was informed by experience and lack of experience. In the summer of 1936, at age eighteen, I spent a month at Fort Oglethorpe, Georgia, as a part of the Civilian Military Training Corps (CMTC). In three years, Germany would invade Poland. Two years before, war between Japan and China had ignited. It was at a time when our country followed a policy of isolationism. The memories of the Great Depression and a tragic and bloody World War I were fresh. CMTC was Roosevelt's way of incrementally preparing for war at a time when war was on the horizon.

It was horse-cavalry training, and with that taste of army life, I was sure I did not want to join the army. Though I had never been in an airplane, I appreciated the risks associated with falling a great distance. The air force held no attraction for me, so I settled on the navy, though I had never seen an ocean!

WARREN, OHIO

Completing my junior year at LMU, I returned to Ohio—this time to Warren, Ohio—for summer employment at the Copperweld Steel Company, about ten to fifteen miles from the home of my aunt and uncle, where I resumed occupancy of my old room. War has a way of creating job opportunities at home as military ranks swell. The Copperweld plant is permanently closed now, but then, we were at war, and there was plenty of work available. I was assigned the job of operating a large electric crane. Running the length of the mill, it rolled along tracks on the walls on each side, high above the floor where the rolling facilities were in operation, it hauled enormous loads of steel. As the new guy, I was surprised to have this assignment. I shared travel expenses with two electricians who, each day, drove from the Youngstown area. I remember the driver as a crusty old Welshman afflicted with a perpetually bad temper.

That summer, I had the requirement of a second year of a foreign language facing me before I could earn my bachelor of arts degree, with one year of German behind me. However, LMU was no longer offering German, so fortified with two years of high-school Spanish four years in my past, I purchased Spanish language books to memorize vocabulary in the spare moments when my crane was not in service. I passed the class and received my BA; in some part, thanks to a summer job with idle time.

GRADUATION

College kids at LMU wasted valuable hours thinking about sex. No news there, and I am sure this was not limited to LMU. This is not a criticism. College is a good place for that to take place, a safe place, especially on smaller college campuses. The students are of marrying age, and there is much to learn about each other before making that commitment. Living with other guys, other personalities with their own habits and quirks, and meeting the academic and social requirements of college contributed to the person I finally became. However, it was not until I reached my late twenties that I felt like a mature adult. In fact, the shaping and reshaping, the evolving, seems to have continued long after Rhondda and I were married.

Classes at LMU were growing smaller and smaller as the LMU boys continued to volunteer for service. The army air force seemed to be the most popular branch. It had established an introductory training program on the LMU campus, drawing thirty to forty young men for classwork, which was complemented by basic flight training over in Middlesboro, Kentucky. Bill Covey preceded me as Professor Johnson's lab assistant. He had graduated from LMU a year earlier and was teaching in that program.

Soon, the boys who had completed their officer training programs began to matriculate back to LMU before assignment to active duty. This included Ben Click, a fraternity brother, who showed up in his new second lieutenant's uniform with shiny new air-force bars on his shoulders. He invited three of us to dinner at the Little Tunnel Inn, a local place that served food and spirits, sometimes attracting a rowdy crowd. It was a great evening, but I reached my limit before I knew it, became sick, and hurried out of the Inn to Ben's car. I was an inexperienced drinker and sitting on the running board, the contents of my stomach erupted and spilled to the ground. Like many before me and many after, I swore never to drink again. I did not keep that oath, but I was never a big drinker. Ben returned from the war intact and wearing the insignia of a Colonel.

I first met Becky Welch at Fort Oglethorpe in the Civilian Military Training Corp in 1936. At LMU, he was also in Sigma Pi Beta, and he also returned to campus in 1941, but with a wife, the former Polly Ford. A very good dancer, she had been my date to a few parties on campus. The two of them were wonderful people, but their marriage was cut short when Becky did not return from the war. On his return from a mission, his B-25 Bomber crashed in Southern Italy, leaving behind Polly and a young son. I saw Polly a few times after the war and enjoyed a few dates. Ultimately, she returned to her home in Jellico, Tennessee, directly west of Harrogate, and remarried.

I left LMU with many lasting impressions and friendships and corresponded with classmates for years to come. Occasionally, a face or a name comes to mind, and I remember good times when I was young and the promise of the future beckoned all of us.

ENTERING THE NAVY, 1943

After graduation in June of 1943, the navy wasted no time. I received my orders to report to the Midshipman School at Columbia University in September, leaving me three months with nothing to do. A little more than twenty miles from family, Oakridge, Tennessee, was home to a big government project shrouded in mystery. I applied for a job and was quickly hired and put to work on a Monday morning in Y-12, one of the divisions of the project. I was a draftsman, drawing architectural plans for buildings to be constructed on the site. The job was not technical. I stored and retrieved drawings as directed. The various divisions were probably sequestered so that no one saw the whole picture. Nevertheless, with the opportunity to study the drawings and having an undergraduate science degree, I tried to figure out what was to be made there. I didn't.

My temporary employment in Oak Ridge ended in September. I left my job, packed my bag lightly and, with my government voucher, I purchased a train ticket for travel from Knoxville to New York City, where my orders directed me to the naval training program at Columbia University. The train coach was crowded. They always were during the war. As we rolled our way north, through Richmond, then Washington, making various stops, new passengers found there were no seats for them. I saw more and more men my age, guessing correctly they were all bound for Columbia University. Our travel took us through New Jersey, and from time to time on my way to becoming a navy midshipman, I caught my first glimpses of the Atlantic Ocean. Finally, the train pulled into Pennsylvania

Station. The navy had busses waiting to deliver us to Columbia University at 116th Street. We expected hours of checking in and a brief medical exam, and that is what met our arrival. I was assigned to Room 809 of Johnson Hall, a tall building designed as a women's dormitory. There I found my roommate, Kenneth Pollard, another LMU chemistry major.

It was my first time in NYC. Through the windows of our eighth floor corner room, we could see busy Harlem looming below the terminus of 116th Street. Only a month earlier, a Black woman named Marjorie Polite had checked into the Braddock Hotel, about ten blocks from my room on campus. Although the hotel had declined since it's halcyon days in the twenties, the hotel lounge was popular with Black celebrities and musicians, including Billie Holiday, Ella Fitzgerald, Dizzy Gillespie, and Malcolm Little, later known as Malcolm X. Finding the accommodations unsatisfactory, she checked out and asked the elevator operator to return her dollar tip. A row ensued and matters hastily deteriorated. A Black soldier in the military police named Robert Bandy, there to take his mother to dinner, was shot by a White police officer when Bandy objected to the disorderly conduct arrest of police. Though the wound was superficial, the rumor spread that Bandy had succumbed to his injuries spread through the community like a virus, becoming racial tinder for igniting a riot. Mayor LaGuardia managed to quell the unrest the following day, but only after several were killed and hundreds were injured. The event inspired William Henry Johnson, a son of Florence, South Carolina, who had moved to the city, to paint *Moon Over Harlem*, which now hangs in the Smithsonian American Art Museum.

There was little time allowed for us to settle into our rooms. We reported next to the nearby barber, following a long line of midshipmen into a barber's chair for a haircut that would be over in moments. Most of us chuckled at our appearance as we put on our navy caps, but not all of us. Classes began on our first day, and the first class for my platoon was aircraft recognition. The image of a German or Japanese aircraft was flashed on the screen, and the students were expected to recognize it instantly. The next day, the instructor began his class with an examination on the planes seen the previous day. To be put "on the tree" meant that the midshipman was denied liberty and a chance to take in New York, instead to stand watch. Unfortunately, my medical exam from the previous day indicated that I had an elevated blood pulse. Hardly unexpected, but I was being checked again during the first day of plane recognition training; so when my plane recognition skills were tested the following day, I failed and landed "on the tree." It was my first and last time.

Khaki shirts and trousers were the uniform during the week, but on liberty weekend and required church services, we wore navy blues. We were a spectacle for New Yorkers each Sunday evening as we marched to and from nearby Riverside Church on 116th Street, a grand and highly ornamented cathedral with vaulted ceilings. Each Sunday people lined the streets as our ranks filed past, singing navy songs. Each Sunday, the service was concluded with officers and midshipmen rising and joining in the solemn and forbidding hymn that sent us from the sanctuary, again forming ranks for the march back down 116th street.

> *Stand navy out to sea,*
> *Fight our battle cry*
> *We'll never change our course,*
> *So vicious foe steer shy-y-y-y.*
> *Roll out the TNT,*
> *Anchors aweigh.*
> *Sail on to victory*
> *And sink their bones to Davy Jones, hooray!*
>
> *Anchors aweigh, my boys,*
> *Anchors aweigh.*
> *Farewell to foreign shores,*
> *We sail at break of day-ay-ay-ay.*
> *Through our last night ashore,*

Drink to the foam
Until we meet once more.
Here's wishing you a happy voyage home.

Blue of the mighty deep
Gold of God's great sun.
Let these our colors be
Till all of time be done, done, done, done.
On seven seas, we learn
Navy's stern call
Faith, courage, service *true,*
With honor, over honor, over all.

I later learned that Doris Sopkin, a Florence, South Carolina neighbor, was among the crowds lining the street near Riverside as a young girl.

Classes resumed in the morning. Courses in addition to aircraft recognition included navigation, fire control, naval science and tactics, a smattering of general naval information, plus physical training, exercises, running, and heavy calisthenics. We ran or marched from class to class and would end the exercise period with push-ups. Lined up according to height, Strawn Taylor from Kentucky was lean and light. When the rest of us were exhausted, he continued to pump up and down. He also ended up in PT boats. After four months, we were to emerge from midshipman school as ensigns. It was a hurried program. The war was waiting for us.

Beneath the broad steps to the Columbia University Library on 116th, we drilled for hours, sometimes with rifles. The drill instructors were usually young ensigns or lieutenant JGs, who had usually not yet seen any sea duty. It was a rotating responsibility—each midshipman getting his chance at directing the drills, calling cadence, and moving his company by voice and hand signals, though most had never marched in rank, much less given orders. What could go wrong? There were massive pileups when crossing paths with another marching company, drawing the ire of the drill instructor while those of us to the rear struggled to contain our enjoyment at the misfortune of the luckless midshipman who failed to stop or turn his troops.

Though the immediate trajectory for my life was into a world war in a faraway place, my four months at Columbia, September through December of 1943, were not unpleasant. I was able to roam the streets of New York, visit Broadway for a few shows, and ride the subway for a nickel. Otherwise, we ate, studied, drilled, and slept—all to the neglect of a social life. That's not why we were there. During my final two years at LMU, I would have referred to Mary Helen Carter as my girlfriend, but when she came to NYC, it was not to see me, but to get a job. It was just as well. Midshipman school left me little time for someone which time, distance, and the war would make a former girlfriend.

The subway was a quick and inexpensive way to get to Forty-Second Street, and the excitement of being a part of the spectacle that was New Year's Eve at Time Square in 1943. For a kid from East Tennessee, it was electrifying. I came upon a midshipman from my company, a short and thick Texan, who gave the initial impression of being shy. Maybe it was the charged atmosphere, but his quiet façade vanished as we walked or stood on Forty-Second Street and the celebrants filed by. When unaccompanied pairs or groups of girls passed, he shamelessly approached them with a doomed pick-up line. Maybe it was the uniforms, but it worked. I was astonished at the number of giggling girls who stopped for conversation. Maybe I was the shy one.

Fast-forward to New Year's Day of 1945. I was again in Time Square. I had survived the South Pacific and had been in Cuba for the last four months on navy business. Again, strolling among the revelers, I came upon the incongruous sight of a young naval officer walking down Broadway with a finely tooled saddle over his shoulder. I recognized him from my days in the South Pacific. He explained he was taking it "back to Texas." The same evening, I recognized JC Dunn, a submariner just in from the Atlantic. JC was an across the street neighbor in Harriman, whose sister, Josephine Kelly, would live in neighboring Dillon, South Carolina, during my Florence years.

I was soon part of a commissioning ceremony, with a thousand other midshipmen at a nearby Catholic cathedral. It was December of 1943, and midshipman school had drawn to an end. The future ensigns in the program had elected their choice of duty and were interviewed for their chosen positions. Serving as a junior officer in the crew of a large ship or landing barge held no interest for me, but the independence and informality of Motor Torpedo duty appealed to me. I interviewed with officers from the PT Boat School at Melville, Rhode Island. Beyond midshipman school, my resume included a bachelor of arts degree, high school football, my CMTC training, and my interest in swimming, fishing, and the water in general, satisfied what I think was a low bar during wartime. I left the commissioning ceremony an ensign, and walking away from the ceremony, a noncommissioned officer raised his hand in salute. I returned the salute and handed him one dollar, observing the navy's "first salute" tradition. I received my orders to report to Melville after a nice leave in Harriman.

In two weeks, it was January 1944, and I was again on a train from Knoxville to Melville, Rhode Island, to become a PT boat officer. In those days, train and bus stations were packed with servicemen and civilians trying to carry on with their lives as best as possible. Rationing of gasoline and tires contributed to herding onto public transportation. Consequently, every seat, all the aisle standing room, and even some of the overhead baggage racks were occupied by passengers. I found my place on the unheated platform of the northbound passenger car, wrapped in my heavy navy coat. The lesson that next time I should arrive early to the station steeped through Tennessee and Virginia as I stood outside the warmth of the coach. When we came to a stop and a passenger disembarked, I raced for the vacated seat before new passengers boarded. It is easy to conceive that wartime crowding of public transportation contributed to President Eisenhower's decision to champion the construction of the Interstate highway system, perhaps as a young army officer in 1919, traveling in a convoy on the Lincoln Highway, the first highway to cross the country. Today, it is difficult to imagine this country without Interstate highways.

MELVILLE, RHODE ISLAND

A train bound for Boston from New York got me to Providence, Rhode Island, where a gray navy bus waited to take new students the twenty or so miles to Melville on Narragansett Bay. The base was located on the eastern side of the bay. Reminding me now of Gomer Pyle's Camp Henderson, there were rows of Quonset huts, steel buildings with rounded tops. Named for Quonset Point on the western side of the bay where they were first built, they offered little insulation against the unforgiving winter weather. The potbellied coal stove located in the center of the room struggled to keep the space comfortable. After the usual processing, I was assigned to one of the half barrel-like buildings. There were perhaps ten bunks, the potbellied stove and little else in the way of furnishings. This was to be home until March 1944. It was midwinter, and the New England cold had descended, depositing a blanket of snow that remained throughout my stay. Deposits of coal to the stove were frequent.

Other than sleeping, little time was spent in the Quonset huts. Classes and short nightly training cruises on the bay and surrounding waters required most of our time. We would race out into the bay, often through Buzzards Bay as far as Nantucket and Martha's Vineyard and sometimes Falmouth. We rose from our bunks early, ate breakfast in the mess hall, and assembled for instructions.

BASE TO "AB" BUOY VIA "12A" BUOY & B.R.L.S.

(Chart 466A Var. 14-30 W.)

FROM	TO	C/Mag.	C/True	Naut. Miles	Reciprocal C/Mag.	C/True	Yards Abeam	C/C When Nav. Aid is:
Nun 14	12A	265.0	250.5	0.65	085.0	070.5	Port 150	12A Abeam to port
12A	Fairway	214.5	200.0	3.55	034.5	020.0	Port clse abd	
Fairway	8A	214.5	200.0	1.2	034.5	020.0	Port 500	
8A	4B	214.5	200.0	1.45	034.5	020.0	Port 100	4B Abeam to port
4B	3A	186.0	171.5	0.84	006.0	351.5	Stbd. clse abd	3A abeam to starboard
3A	1	219.0	204.5	0.15	039.0	024.5	Stbd. clse abd	1 Abeam to starboard
1	P	239.0	224.5	0.8	059.0	044.5	Stbd. clse abd	"P" Abeam to Starboard
P	N	228.0	213.5	1.1	048.0	033.5	Stbd. clse abd	"N" Abeam to Starboard
N	BRLS	199.0	184.5	1.6	019.0	004.5	Port 200	B.R.L.S. Abeam to port
BRLS	AB	179.0	164.5	5.55	359.0	344.0		

DIRECTIONS

Point of departure 300 yards outboard of Nun 14 on base channel course.

1. Thence from point of departure c/c to 265.0 mag. for 0.65 miles leaving buoy 12A abeam to port 150 yards.
2. C/c to 214.5 mag. for 3.55 miles leaving fairway buoy abeam to port close aboard.
3. Continue on c-214.5 mag. for 1.2 miles leaving buoy 8A abeam to port distance 500 yards.
4. Continue on c-214.5 mag. for 1.45 miles leaving buoy 4B abeam to port distance 100 yards.
5. C/c to 186.0 mag. for 0.84 miles leaving buoy 3A abeam to starboard, close aboard.
6. C/c to 219.0 mag. for .15 miles leaving bell 1 abeam to starboard close aboard.
7. C/c to 239.0 mag. for 0.8 miles leaving fairway "P" abeam to starboard, close aboard.
8. C/c to 228.0 mag. for 1.1 miles leaving fairway "N" abeam to starboard, close aboard.
9. C/c to 199.0 mag. for 1.6 miles leaving Brenton Reef Light Ship abeam to port, distance 200 yards.
10. C/c to 179.0 mag. for 5.55 miles to a point bearing 000.0 true from buoy AB distance 200 yards. (This point will be used as a departure point for all open water navigation.)

Patrol instructions for underway exercises in
Motor Torpedo Patrol Training

Wearing underway gear, we spent the day performing training exercises on the choppy water, with a cold wind and mist blowing in our faces. By the time we returned to base, the spray would have frozen to our outer gear. They are called motor torpedo patrol boats, but in the South Pacific, they were used principally as gun boats. That said, in training, we fired one torpedo. Another was not fired again from any vessel in my South Pacific squadron until the Battle of Leyte Gulf, when one of my squadron's boats was credited with sinking a Japanese cruiser.

The atmosphere in the Quonset hut was light. On turning in, we stoked the coal-burning stove and, with long johns and heavy woolen socks, slid beneath the blankets. A bit of banter would follow, sometimes a ribald story and laughter from the eight or ten trainees before falling asleep. Reveille sounded at 6:00 a.m., and we opened our eyes to another day of training. Ensign Sloat from Wisconsin took it upon himself to rouse us and would spring from his bed and dance from one bed to another, singing and shouting.

My training in Melville lasted only two months, and at best, it was only an introductory experience. I did very little boat handling. While the weather there did nothing to prepare me for the South Pacific, the night patrols were valuable. All our patrols in the South Pacific were at night. We did learn the specifications of our boats, but frankly, there wasn't a great deal we needed to learn that would not be quickly acquired when we went into combat duty.

There were officer's clubs in Providence, Newport, and Melville. I took the opportunity to visit each a couple of times, but a party at the officer's club (or mess hall) in Melville stands out because Lieutenant Commander John D. Bulkeley was there. He was famous as the skipper of PT-41 in Squadron 3, who had rescued General Douglas McArthur, his family, and staff from the Corregidor Islands on May of 1942. In tempestuous waters, a crewman that night remembered the experience on board as a "combination of bucking bronco and a wallowing tub." Within months, W. L. White had written a best-selling account of that mission, *They Were Expendable.* Jack Kennedy, whose family home in Hyannis was seventy to eighty miles away, was "recruited" to motor torpedo service by Bulkeley and trained at Melville and was very possibly at the party as well. His recognition came a few months earlier on the night of August 1, 1943. His engine idling on open water in anticipation of a rendezvous, a Japanese destroyer emerged from the darkness and split the PT in half. He gathered his crew on the plywood remains of the boat and led them to an island, towing his burned engineer behind him to the beach three miles away. Not infrequently, people learning of my navy service in the South Pacific ask if I ever met Kennedy. Maybe.

Finding Squadron 7

My two months at Melville completed, I got my orders to report to San Francisco—there to find transportation to motor torpedo boat Squadron 7. Before boarding the Union Pacific train for California, I stopped in New York for a visit with Mary Helen and her aunt. The next day, the aunt treated me to a steak dinner at a restaurant near Penn Station before boarding the train for the Chicago leg of my journey to find Squadron 7. The navy provided for my first Pullman bedroom, the second bed occupied by an army captain. It was the first and last sleeper compartment ever provided to me by the navy.

My ultimate arrival at Squadron 7 dominated my thoughts, but I enjoyed the comfort of travelling by train. We made a stop in North Platte, Nebraska, at the confluence of the North and South Platt Rivers, once famous as the home of William Frederick Cody, known as "Buffalo Bill" Cody. Passengers were allowed to stretch their legs, walking around the station. The country had been at war since Pearl Harbor, a galvanizing moment in our history. The North Platte locals, anxious to do their part, had set out tables loaded with food for the passengers, military, and civilian alike. Their hospitality made a lasting impression on me.

The wide open countryside of the Heartland was in sharp contrast to the hills, ridges, and plateau surrounding Harriman and what I had seen of New England. We finally pulled into the station in Oakland, where we took the ferry over to San Francisco. I reported in and was directed to a small hotel near Market Street, with a stipend for food. There would be little time to explore the city. Each morning, I climbed into a cable car at 8:30 a.m. and reported at 9:00 a.m. to a large indoor swimming pool. All officers destined for the South Pacific received training in swimming and "abandon-ship" procedures. The swimming instructor was a highly qualified and well-known woman named Ann Elizabeth Curtis. It was the early spring of 1944, and she was an eighteen-year-old freshman at the Berkeley campus of the University of California, having already collected medals in dozens of competitions, including the prestigious Sullivan Award, given to the most outstanding amateur athlete in America. She was the first woman and the first swimmer to receive the honor. After the war, she would win two gold medals and one silver medal in the 1948 London Olympics. Between her personal training and college classes, she could not have had a great deal of time, but she had a personal motivation to do her part for the war effort. In the preceding November, her father, a marine captain, was involved in the Battle of Tarawa, a small atoll about one thousand miles east of New Guinea. It is regarded as the toughest battle in marine corps history. About one thousand marines were killed, including her father.

The officers in the class, perhaps fifty to seventy-five of us, were required to don a kapok life jacket, climb a ladder high into the top of the building, and walk to the end of a diving board. Arms crossed, firmly grasping the life jacket under each arm, we "abandoned ship," jumping to the water's surface far below. It was daunting, and many of the young terrified officers walked to the end of the board and stood frozen. With the advantage of not being at the front of the line, I determined that when my turn came, I would cross my arms, grab my vest, and jump with no hesitation, allowing no time to think about it. Though abandoning ship was not a part of my plan for the war, I walked to the end of the board and jumped without looking down at the water or breaking stride, striking the water with a bone-shaking impact.

Built in 1943, the Cape Newenham—417 feet 9 inches overall length,
60 feet beam, and 27 feet draft—the ship was capable of doing fourteen
knots and carried up to 1,830 passengers and 99,260 cubic feet of cargo.
It was operated by American Mail Line, Ltd. during World War II.

My visit to San Francisco ended after a couple of weeks, when
I received orders to board the USS *Cape Newenham*, a troop ship at
the navy docks in Oakland. A truck arrived at my hotel, delivering a
giant canvas bag too large to reach around. It contained all the personal equipment I would need for going to war, a pith helmet, brown
high-top marine boots, mosquito netting, a Colt .45 pistol with
ammunition, a metal combat helmet, a poncho, and other items for
surviving the war and the tropics.

OFFICER ROSTER
-SS CAPE NEWENHAM-

Date: 9 March 1944
No. 1405

C O N F I D E N T I A L

The Naval Personnel listed below have been directed to report for detachment as of 9 March 1944, for transportation furnished via SS CAPE NEWENHAM destined for UROM.

NO.	NAME	RANK		DESTINATION	DUTY
		LIEUTENANT COMMANDER			
1.	JOHNSON, Ira	Lt.Comdr. SC-V(S)	USNR	KDUR	24thNAVCONSRG
		LIEUTENANT			
2.	TIGERMAN, Louis	Lt. O-V(S)	USNR	KDUR	USS RIGEL
		ENSIGN			
3.	MOORE, M. R.	Ens. D-V(G)	USNR	KDUR	MTBRONSEVENTHFLT
4.	PENDOCK, Charles Edward	Ens. D-V(G)	USNR	KDUR	COMMTBRONSEVENTHFLT
5.	REDFERN, Charles T.	Ens. D-V(G)	USNR	KDUR	COMMTBRONSEVENTHFLT
6.	RICHARDS, Gene (n)	Ens. SC-V(G)	USNR	KDUR	C.B. #60
7.	ROBERTSON, William Hall	Ens. D-V(G)	USNR	KDUR	MTBRONSEVENTHFLT
8.	SCHWAIGHART, Paul F., Jr.	Ens. SC-V(G)	USNR	KDUR	LCT (5) FLOT 7
9.	SCOTT, James P.	Ens. SC-V(G)	USNR	KDUR	LST GROUP 19
10.	SHEPHERD, Robert Neal	Ens. A-V(S)	USNR	KDUR	FAIRWING 17 HEDRON
11.	SHREVE, Robert H.	Ens. D-V(G)	USNR	KDUR	MTBRONSEVENTHFLT
12.	SMITH, Walter Douglas	Ens. D-V(G)	USNR	KDUR	MTBRONSEVENTHFLT
		WARRANT OFFICER			
13.	PLAUSHAK, John	Carp	USN	KDUR	USS RIZAR

Tranship from UROM to KDUR.

Lt.(jg) L. F. Marshall, USNR
Loading Officer

C O N F I D E N T I A L
CC: Port Director - UROM
Port Director - KDUR
Bulers
General Files   GRAND TOTAL _____
Surface Transp. File
Comdr. Armstrong
C. O. of Troops
Fleet Records   DESTINATION & DUTY CHECKED _____

The roster of the thirteen US Navy officers aboard
the Cape Newenham, three of whom are assigned to
MTBRONSEVENTHFLT duty (motor torpedo boat Seventh
Fleet), including Ensign Shreve (11) and Ensign Smith (12).

The following day, I was met in the hotel lobby by navy seamen, who assisted me with depositing my luggage in a navy vehicle. Arriving at the docks in Oakland, I joined perhaps 1,500 soldiers and sailors, and a dozen or more navy officers, all of us standing at ease, surrounded by our gear, all waiting to board the Cape Newenham bound for various destinations in the South Pacific. Stacked four high, my bunk was third from the bottom, with Bob Shreve below me. The challenge of just getting to it meant I would spend little time there. Filled with twenty-five to thirty officers below the rank of navy lieutenant commander or army major, our "cabin" was a twenty-five-by-thirty-foot room on the third or fourth deck below the main deck. To reach fresh air and sunshine, I scaled several of the hybrid ship ladders/stairs found on ships.

The service branches were somewhat segregated aboard ship. I saw little of the army officers who had supervision of their troops. Having no navy personnel, for which we were responsible, navy officers were free to explore the ship. Mess in the evening was usually followed by the dozen or so navy officers gathering topside under the tropical stars for conversation. The ship's prow pushed through the sea at six knots, in a southwesterly direction, destinations undisclosed to its passengers. Troop movement was closely held intelligence.

A chief warrant officer was among our group. With many years of navy service, he regaled us with stories collected over the years. C.T. Redfern from Enid, Oklahoma, was over six feet tall and well over two hundred pounds. He entertained us with stories, real and fictional, usually about his many romances. I last saw him in Newport in 1945. He was in the company of a charming local girl he later married.

We crossed the equator, and the fact was given a muted recognition on the Cape Newenham. We were handed certificates signed by *Davey Jones, Neptunus Rex*, and, on this voyage, by Captain Lewis. Traditionally commemorative of a sailor's first crossing, it is attended by "pollywogs," the initiates, and by "shellbacks," the veteran sailors. Sometimes called the King Neptune Celebration, it is a favorite on cruise ships, and I was reminded of it later on a Quantas flight to

Australia with Rhondda and Walt, when the stewardess navigated the aisle with certificates and King Neptune pins.

The average annual temperature at the equator is eighty-eight degrees, due to the direct angle of the sun. A large shower room with no stalls and no freshwater had perhaps ten showerheads available to us anytime. In the hot Pacific, even a saltwater shower could be satisfying, though it left us feeling a bit sticky. The water would sometimes turn off with no warning, so we soon learned to fill our helmets with water before soaping as a precaution.

Eventually, land appeared on the horizon. What appeared to be tree-covered slopes surrounding a harbor, it was probably New Hebrides, an archipelago separated from Australia by the Coral Sea, and neighbored by New Caledonia and the Solomon Islands. After gaining independence from the joint rule of Great Britain and France, it is now called Vanuatu. The navy officer passengers quickly disembarked and moved into temporary quarters, leaving the ship's manifest of army troops to sally forth into the Coral Sea, probably bound for New Guinea to the northwest. For the next four days, we would await passage to our assigned destinations.

A small bay separated our barracks from the main facilities, including the small officer's club surrounded by a tropical forest. Aboard a small barge, we repaired to the club each afternoon. My new friend, Bob Shreve, liked to drink but was not very good at it; getting drunk and losing his equilibrium after about four drinks, he regularly needed help getting back to the barracks.

It was from the club on the third day that a colossal hospital ship came into view in the harbor. As it closed in on the docks, I recognized the ship. I had met a navy nurse in Newport who was assigned to nursing duties aboard. A boat filled with navy nurses was lowered to the surface, and to my surprise, there she was. Although we had only a couple of dates in Newport, we fell into each other's arms, like a scene from a movie. The moment was underscored by the sheer coincidence of finding each other again in the South Pacific. The next couple of hours were spent drinking, dancing, and in animated conversation. When it was time for the girls to retreat to the hospital ship, I gallantly stepped forward to lift her from the dock to the waiting boat. With one foot on the dock and one on the boat, she was in my arms as the gap between the dock and the untethered boat grew. We both comically tumbled into the drink. The other nurses and my navy buddies got a good laugh that was not shared by the hospital boat crew hurling derision at me as I splashed in the water, retrieving my pith helmet. I struggled onto the dock with what remained of my dignity and joined in the laughter. My wristwatch never worked again but always reminded me of that moment. There were times that I saw the hospital ship in other harbors, but not the nurse.

The next day, a Dutch tanker entered the harbor, and with my friends, I went aboard carrying the canvas bag delivered to me in San Francisco before departing on the USS *Cape Newenham*. It was a clean ship, and the food was reasonably good. We had no work assignments and spent our time playing cards, reading, and traversing the catwalks at middeck with expansive views of the ocean. The routine continued for some six days before we entered another island harbor. I parted from the friends I had made since leaving San Francisco and, without going ashore, transferred to an English frigate, a fighting ship smaller than a destroyer. Passing west in the night through the Solomon Sea, fully clothed, I slept fitfully on a hard couch. Dawn broke, and I ascended to the deck to see the frigate slipping into another island harbor. Drawing closer, I could make out the PT boats secured to docks that ran out from the beach. Planes were taking off from an airstrip that ran parallel to the shoreline. I had arrived at Finschhafen on the east coast of New Guinea, north of Australia. For the moment, it was home to Squadrons 7 and 8, each with twelve boats. Reporting to Commander Robert Leeson, I was assigned to PT-138.

I walked along the dock until I found PT-138 resting quietly in the hot sunshine with a crew that appeared to have nothing to do. I met the skipper, who was being rotated back to the States, and the executive officer who would then take the skipper's place as I would succeed him. I can see their faces today but cannot pull up their names. As in my case, the ranks of PT officers are usually filled with ensigns and lieutenants junior grade (JGs), immediately after completing motor torpedo boat basic training.

Only one night would be spent in Finschhafen. By late afternoon of the following day, the engines of both squadrons fired up, and the PTs followed a heading that took us around the northern coast of New Guinea and west toward Madang, Wewak, Aitape, and the Sepik River of Margaret Mead fame. She was the American cultural anthropologist, who famously said, "Always remember, you are absolutely unique, just like everyone else." I took my turn at the helm for the first time that night, having the experience from Narragansett Bay of staying in proper formation with the other boats at around thirty knots. It was early morning when we passed between small islands to enter a well-protected cove at Aitape. The water was still. From there, we would patrol for the next four-and-a-half months. The New Guinea coastline there is a straight line of sand, edged by the ocean on one side and by palm trees on the island side, oven hot during the day until the sun drops below the horizon at night. Our tender was a converted Landing Ship Tank (LST), designed to deliver tanks, equipment, cargo, supplies, and troops directly on a beach. It dropped anchor at a central spot in the bay, and the PTs followed suit at safe distances. The LST also had a mess service for officers where I frequently took my meals and our boat's cook would visit each day, returning with food for the crew.

On our second night at Aitape, my boat was ordered into patrol duty. With PT-138 leading, PT-137 joined the patrol, and we left our quiet anchorage in the late afternoon. Malcolm was the name of the PT-137 skipper, and his executive officer was Bob Warner. Our course was due east, along a ten-mile stretch of the north coast of New Guinea, retracing our course of two days earlier. The boats planed at twenty-five to thirty knots, and we were in position by sundown. Within one hundred to two hundred yards of the beach, we muffled our engines and began the slow eight-to-ten-knot patrol. It was quiet, only the muffled engines could be heard. At around 9:00 p.m., I made my way to the bow, finding sixteen-year-old George manning a 37 mm cannon acquired from the air force. George had falsified his age to his recruiter. All the men were on their guns; each trained on the beach and prepared to fire if the enemy revealed their positions by firing on us or if Japanese barges were sighted. From the quiet beach, bathed in moonlight, gun fire erupted, and tracers were coming at us. George's 37 mm thumped with return fire, accompanied by two 20 mm cannons and two .50-caliber machine guns staffed by other gunners. PT-138 completed its pass and turned to port, allowing PT-137 to fall in and make its pass. No further gunfire came from the beach, and after a second run, our patrol continued. The explosions of our shells mingled with the sound of trees felled on the island. Our patrol ended with the rising sun. It was the first time anyone shot at me. You remember that kind of thing.

The PTs were radar equipped, and we monitored the screen constantly. PTs were comparatively small, fast, and considered expendable vessels for short-range scouting. Armed with torpedoes, cannons, and machine guns, our primary mission was to cut enemy supply lines and harass enemy forces. The Japanese barges stayed close to shore, indistinguishable from the shoreline at night, but on the radar, moving objects against the stationary coast were revealed during our midnight patrols along the island coasts.

The two squadrons, 7 and 8, continued the nightly patrols along eighty to one hundred miles of the New Guinea coast, from Aitape

eastward past Wewak, for over four-and-a-half months, engine muf-
flers on, and all eyes and ears alert for signs or sounds of barges and
other Japanese traffic. Furnished with fine binoculars, we surveyed
our surroundings. Peripheral vision was important. The patrol ended
at daylight, and the two boats would head out to sea and race back
to the base. The race signaled the cook to prepare breakfast for the
crew unless weather and chop were too much. Then we had coffee
and breakfast waited for our return.

The PTs were to be on constant alert and prepared to go at a
moment's notice. Our first responsibility on our return to the harbor at Aitape was to refuel. The Packard gasoline engines, ranging
from 1450 to 1750 horsepower, guzzled one hundred octane fuels.
Refueling was followed by cleaning the deck, reloading guns as
needed, and any other task necessary to standing readiness. Done,
the crew raised a canvas awning that covered the deck and made
dockside sleeping more comfortable. The nightly patrols were long,
sometimes testing our nerves, and sleep was welcome.

The Japanese Army in New Guinea was isolated from the
mother country in 1944. The PT boats were fulfilling their mission.
Big ships had no chance of getting through our lines to bring provisions to their stranded army. Some submarines may have made it
but could not have provided much in the way of supplies for their
besieged army. The US Army engaged the Japanese on the mainland around Aitape. In the harbor, we could hear the thunderous
firing of heavy guns from time to time. Under cover of night to avoid
detection by US and Australian planes, the Japanese attempted to
move supplies along the coast on barges. The PTs were built for the
job, but not without risk. The barges were typically well-armed and
effective in battles with the PT boats. It was not infrequent that we
encountered gunfire on our patrols, sometimes just a burst or two,
but it always provoked a rain of hell from our boats. Twice, PT-138
sustained some damage. On one such occasion, Commander Leeson
was on board, a rotating weekly practice of the commander. We were
patrolling the beach near the entrance to Wewak, along the western
side of the long cape that stretches north and south in front of that
harbor. Making a pass with our starboard side exposed to the beach,

gunfire came from the island. At the first sound of enemy guns, our gunners returned fire. At the helm, I held course, with PT-137 at our stern, in position to begin firing. I turned to port to prepare for another run. "Cosmo's been hit!" a crewman shouted from the stern. I turned, and in the dark night, I saw Cosmo motionless on the deck. Pulling away from the beach, I examined his wound with a flashlight in hand. A large caliber bullet had passed through him, leaving a gaping wound as it exited. Cosmo Treva, gunner's mate from Newton, Massachusetts, was dead. It was his third patrol on the third boat of his service. The third patrols of his previous two attachments had met with disaster, one sunk and the other was severely damaged. A subscriber to the belief that bad things happen in threes, the numbers were a dark and disquieting prediction. He had shared his apprehension with me the day before leaving the dock.

Cosmo's body was prepared for burial on the tender. At mid-morning of the next day, with most of the crew accompanying the body, a barge carried us across the bay to the mainland of Aitape. There, a newly cleared area, a short distance from the beach, had been designated as the American cemetery. An army chaplain presided over a brief service, an army detail fired their guns into the air, and the body was lowered into the grave. I overheard Commander Leeson's remark to the Squadron Exec, "I would prefer burial at sea." I did not share his preference. A subdued crew returned to PT-138. I never learned if Cosmo's remains were left there in that desolate cemetery or returned to Newton, Massachusetts. I have hoped to find my way back to Aitape and that lonely place to honor his memory, but the grave may no longer be there. A large undersea landslide in 1998 caused a severe tsunami that hit the coast at Aitape, killing upwards of 2,700 people.

After losing Cosmo, our patrols continued unabated, and it was not long before we were again engaging the Japanese, just east of Wewak. I was at the helm when we spotted barges moving along the shore. Spinning the wheel quickly to turn our starboards to the barges, we opened up with all guns, each boat making two passes. Coming out of the second pass, I heard swearing and turned to see the machinist's mate who operated the 20 mm cannon. He was attempting to lift the spring-loaded drum holding the shells for his gun from its position. A round from one of the barges had struck it, setting it on fire, threatening an explosion. Finally wrestling it free, he tossed the burning drum into the sea. The rest of the boat was examined for damage after the patrol. Four shells had struck the starboard side, entering the gas tank. Thankfully, a low fuel level saved us from a fiery eruption. The machinist was later awarded a medal as well as a purple heart for the shrapnel wounds to his face and shoulders.

On occasion, there were joint patrols with the Australian Air Force, whose night-flying planes located barges and summoned the PT boats by radio to the position. I met a few of the flyers who impressed me as cavalier about their perilous duty.

Four-and-a-half months at Aitape had quickly passed, and the navy decided my combat duty over that time had earned me a break. Commander Leeson called me in. It was my time to go on leave in Sydney, Australia, for two weeks. Climbing aboard my boat, I hastily packed my uniforms, threw in a few cartons of cigarettes, borrowed money from everyone, and reappeared in front of the skipper. I was ready to go.

SYDNEY, AUSTRALIA

It was late September or early October, and spring had come to Sydney. With another officer, Bob Warner from PT-137, I waited for a barge to ferry us from our boats to the mainland. Once deposited on the New Guinea shore, an army jeep driver volunteered to take us to the airstrip. Like all the airstrips in New Guinea, it was paved with coral. Spotting an army C-47 warming up, we joined a dozen young air force pilots also bound for leave in Australia by way of Madang, another airstrip with support facilities.

I don't recall how, but in the weeks preceding leave, I had come into possession of a fifth of bourbon. Waiting for takeoff, it seemed like a good time for a drink. I pulled the bottle from my bag, took a drink, and passed it around to the others—all taking a healthy swig. It came back to me one more time. As the plane began to taxi down the runway, the young pilots moved forward to place their weight over the wings, clearly apprehensive about getting off the ground. Having never flown before and my bourbon bottle empty, I was quite confident that the plane would fly. We were soon on another coral runway in Madang, my first flight a success.

There was no flight out of Madang that afternoon. We would spend the night. Nearby, we found a tent with bunks that had been occupied many times since the sheets and pillowcases had last been washed. No matter, we slept well and awoke the next morning to find a C-47, its engines warming for a flight south to Australia. Along with the two pilots who seemed pleased to have us aboard, Bob Warner and I were the only passengers. South from Madang, we flew over the high mountains of interior New Guinea, and the southern coast of the country came into view, with the Gulf of Papua and the Coral Sea beyond. Over water with no land in sight for some time, the northern coast of Queensland, Australia, finally appeared, and presently, the Great Barrier Reef was below us for mile after mile. The day was coming to an end when we touched down in Townsville, a small country town in northern Queensland that reminded me of the early twentieth-century villages back home. The Ross River and Ross Creek flow into the Great Barrier Reef at Townsville, with the town built on the estuary between them. Castle Hill is the town's most prominent feature by far. A 938-foot monolith of pink granite provides a natural landmark for ships coming to the town's anchorage.

Exiting the plane, we were greeted by a United Service Organization (USO) welcoming station. For the first time in six months, I ate fresh onions, carrots, and other fresh vegetables, and I drank a tall glass of fresh milk, a reprieve from the powdered milk available to us in New Guinea. It is a memory that sticks with me. With our pilots, we went to the Bachelor Officer Quarters (BOQ) at the small airport. In the evening, we strolled through the town, finally landing at an open-air movie house with fans suspended from the ceilings to move the warm air. The movie was an old one.

The next day, with the plane refueled, Bob Warner and I boarded with the pilots for the southward passage to Brisbane, Queensland, Australia, and another refueling and overnight stop before the last leg of the trip. By midafternoon of the following day, we arrived in Sydney, New South Wales, Australia. Warner and I thanked the pilots and left the plane. There were no customs or immigration officials to question us, no baggage screening; there were no checks of any sort. A taxi took us to the Birnley Hotel, which seemed to be reserved for air force and PT officers. We checked in, found our room, and went in search of friends from other squadrons that had preceded us, including Bob Shreve from Wisconsin, who I last saw on the tanker before boarding the British frigate. I would see him again during leave.

It was a routine among PT boat officers on leave in Sydney to immediately follow registration at the Birnley with a trip to a facility managed by the navy to pick up a weekly ration of spirits, which depended on what was available at the time—usually a few bottles of wine, perhaps a fifth of gin or vodka, sometimes bourbon, maybe something else. It was also the practice of navy officers to enjoy Sydney for a week before going to US Navy Headquarters to announce their arrival in the city. That marked the beginning of the two-week leave. When the two weeks elapsed, the officer would return to HQ and be issued orders to find transportation back to his squadron. With orders in hand, he would enjoy another week at the Birnley. At the conclusion of that week, bags packed, the officer would find his way to the airport and a flight north to New Guinea. It amounts to a week to get to Sydney, two weeks of leave, and a week to rejoin the squadron. Not a moment of the four weeks was squandered, and briefly, the war seemed far away.

Liz was a very pretty and a very tall blond American girl serving as the USO representative. Soon after settling into the Birnley, she let us know about a dance at the hotel that night and asked if we wanted dates. "Yes, a blond, about five feet two inches, please," I responded. Sydney girls, and I imagine girls in other Australian leave destinations, saw entertaining the officers as a means to serve the war effort. All of them had jobs, many in war-related positions. They signed on and were invited to parties and dances. Of course, they were entertained as well. The fellows they met were college graduates, and they had answered their nations call and met the demands of military service, at least checking those boxes as determiners of "good company."

A petite five feet two inches, I was quickly charmed by her shapely figure, dark hair, and accent. Rhondda Miller had arrived for the dance. Thank you, Liz. I remember little about that night, but when the band played a tune later made popular by Bing Crosby, "A Little Spanish Town," Rhondda sang softly in my ear.

> In a little Spanish town, 'twas on a night like this,
> Stars were peek-a-booing down, 'twas on a night
>   like this,
> I whispered "Be true to me," and she sighed, "Si, si."

Many skies have turned to gray because we're far
apart,
Many moons have passed away, and she's still in my
heart.
We made a promise and sealed it with a kiss,
In a little Spanish town, 'twas on a night like this.

I asked her out for the following night. In fact, she was my date every evening throughout my leave, except when her job as a signal instructor for the navy got in the way. There were more dances and parties. I visited her home a few times, had tea with Rhondda and her mother in their garden. The Millers, Henry and Lyn, lived at 25 Vaucluse Road, in an upscale Sydney neighborhood with a panoramic view of Sydney Harbor. Rhondda had grown up in a larger house at 58 Hopetoun Avenue that was sold to purchase the Vaucluse home. Rhondda's brother, Ian, had joined the Australian Army and was away, as was her sister, Joyce, who drove a jeep for the US Army. I did not meet either of them until they both later followed Rhondda to the States.

One of the Rockefellers had leased a house in Sydney and made it available to Commander Leeson, who was also on leave. Rhondda was with me at a party in the borrowed mansion. We went to nightclubs, always with a group of navy officer friends and Australian girls. Rhondda remembered helping an overserved Bob Shreve back to the Birnley Hotel from one of those parties in a late-night streetcar, the only transportation we could find at that hour.

With orders to return to my squadron in hand, my leave in Sydney came to an end. It was on our last evening together that she gave me a picture of her in the snow of the Blue Mountains, some fifty miles west of Sydney, skis and poles splayed and laughing at herself.

I have carried it in my wallet every day since. My leave in Sydney was too abbreviated for Rhondda and I to reach a relationship that suggested a future together, though that was its trajectory. It had been a date that I would never forget. There were some words about writing to each other, but no mention of meeting again. So my leave expired, and we said our "goodbyes" late on the night before I would be on a plane back to New Guinea. We did exchange a few letters, but I imagine I might have been difficult to find, and that I missed a few. She once wrote a letter asking about my well-being, having heard that my squadron had engaged in some fierce skirmishes with the Japanese, which was a possibility with every patrol.

It was November of 1944. Warner and I were at the Sydney airport in a C-47 going north to Brisbane, surrounded by a freight of Mazda light bulbs, a product of General Electric. We refueled and set out again for Townsville and another refueling before going on to New Guinea. In the air and leaving Townsville, the young pilots asked if I wanted to fly the plane, another first for me. I took the pilot's seat as the pilot and copilot eased back in the cabin for a smoke. We climbed to an altitude that carried us over the high-island mountains surrounding the harbor, and soon, the Great Barrier Reef was again below us. The pilots smothered their cigarettes and returned to the cockpit, and I found my place in the cabin among the light bulbs. Our course again took us over the Coral Sea and the Bay of Papua and finally to another coral airstrip in Buna, a place where the Australian and US Armies had a year earlier learned tough lessons about jungle warfare, battling the Japanese who had designed and built a strong network of well-concealed defenses. Losses were high. It was the first time the American public was confronted with images of dead American troops. On that day, tropical Buna was quiet and peaceful. We refueled. Flying over the high, tree-covered mountains of New Guinea, we passed over Hollandia. The harbor was football shaped with a small outlet to the sea. In that harbor were assembled hundreds of military ships of all sizes. We were looking at the invasion force that in a few days would land at Tacloban, Leyte, Philippines. It was the beginning of the Battle of Leyte Gulf. In another hour, the plane began its descent to another island runway. We were in Biak in the Schouten Islands of Indonesia. PT-137 and PT-138 were at anchor awaiting our return.

THE BATTLE OF LEYTE GULF

Lasting three days, October 23–26, 1944, it was the largest naval battle of World War II and vies for the largest naval battle in history, involving over two hundred thousand naval personnel. The Japanese Navy was outgunned by the United States' Third and Seventh fleets and Australian forces but, nevertheless, mustered its remaining vessels to repulse the Allied assault. Taking place in four separate main engagements in and around Leyte, it was the first use of organized kamikaze attacks by the Japanese, and the last confrontation between battleships in history.

All PTs refueled and fully provisioned, we left the harbor the second day to join the armada, battleships, cruisers, destroyers, an array of tenders and other ships—all on their way to the invasion of Leyte. We were joined by several other squadrons. At about 1,200 miles, it was the largest movement of PTs under their own power during the war. Operating at a distance from the main fleet, the PTs in the first wave would provide advance notice of the Japanese fleet movement—spotting them on radar, providing their position, strength, and course to the main fleet while converging to attack Japanese naval assets in the hours before US destroyers arrived from the main fleet.

Our squadron took our position in formation behind a larger ship that was our tender. It carried provisions and fuel for the PT boats. We were on a course of 340 degrees, cruising at fifteen knots. In two days, we were in Peleliu in the Palau group of islands, where we anchored offshore in rough water. None of us slept well.

Daybreak came, and we were again underway, in formation and on a 320-degree course.

Our position behind the tender was strategic to refueling. From time to time, a PT would approach the stern of the tender, and a hose would be extended to the trailing boat to refuel it. For seven hundred miles on open sea from Peleliu, we enjoyed calm seas before entering the harbor at Tacloban, Leyte. The first assault on the island had taken place the previous day. Tacloban was in the hands of the US Navy and Army. It was an enormous harbor, lying well-protected on the San Juanico Strait that separated the closely adjacent islands of Leyte and Samar. Hundreds of ships could find safety there from winds and storms. On many occasions in 1944, the harbor was filled with American warships, tankers, and transports.

Although the Japanese on Leyte appeared to be largely defeated, again, I could hear the roar of big guns in the hills for days. There was no quit in the Japanese. Almost every day for weeks, kamikaze planes would attack, always from behind the hills to the west. Predictably arriving before sundown with the bright sun behind them, there were usually just one or two. Our radar would pick them up at forty miles, alarms around the harbor would wail, and sailors scrambled to their guns and cannons. When the planes came into view, the bay would erupt with gunfire, and the planes would break apart and fall into the sea some distance from their likely targets, the bigger boats. Our PT-138 gunners joined in sending a hail of bullets and exploding shells into the air that returned to the water as a rain of shrapnel. If it were not so sad and pathetic, it might have been entertaining. At this point in the war, the Japanese inventory of planes had dwindled along with their experienced pilots. Unsustainable as a strategy for winning the war, kamikazes were relegated to smaller, slower, and older planes. Gunfire came from everywhere in and around the harbor, and the planes were almost never a credible threat to their targets. I once took my turn at the .50-caliber turret to fire at a kamikaze. The plane went down. Somebody hit it, and it was probably not me.

The Philippines are sun-drenched, often mountainous islands covered in palm trees and thick tropical foliage. Tacloban, the capital of Leyte, still had a few buildings standing when I stepped off the boat. On my third day there, I explored some of the buildings, finding one with a room piled high in fencing materials. I picked up a few posters and books written in Japanese and brought them home with me.

Commander Leeson ordered patrols to begin. PT-138 and another boat weighed anchor and pointed south at dusk to patrol the east coast of Leyte to its southern point, where we would slip through the pass at Surigao Strait, now a graveyard for Japanese warships and their crews. Only days before, American battleships of the Seventh Fleet, taking advantage of an egregious tactical error by the Japanese, were able to "cross the T" on the line of enemy vessels, allowing the American ships to broadside the Japanese ships with minimal return fire, sinking nearly all of them, including two of the Japanese battleships. Notably, all but one of the American battleships had been stationed at Pearl Harbor on December 7, 1941 and had been resurrected and readied for their return to service. Once through the strait, traversed by Ferdinand Magellan in 1521, we turned north on the western side of Leyte and proceeded to Ormoc Bay. There were times that we went the other way to get there. The tapering gap of water between Leyte and Samar was large enough for our PTs to pass for patrols to the western side of Leyte. In some places, it looked like a river but was wide and deep enough to accommodate our relatively shallow three-feet-and-six-inches draft and our twenty-feet-and-eight-inches beam. At the other end, we entered the Visayan Sea, northwest of Leyte and south of Luzon. We often took that route and circled south to the western side of Leyte and into Ormoc Bay.

It was all new to us. The army had only landed two days earlier, and the strength of Japanese forces being pushed out of Tacloban was uncertain. Filipinos on the small islands came out to meet us in their outrigger canoes (*bangka*), bringing bananas and other native produce to trade for T-shirts and other supplies with which we were amply provisioned. Their clothes were tattered and sometimes appeared to be nothing more than patches of cloth stitched together. Their need was so apparent we did not barter. That early morning stop at the small islands in Leyte's south became routine in the following two months. Patrolling further south, along the northern coast of Mindanao, about a mile from shore, we saw many small fishing boats with small contained fires aboard for cooking.

Referred to as the "Tokyo Express," no barge traffic was encountered around Leyte. With the Japanese Army all but completely routed, there was no one left to supply. Their air attacks came frequently but did little damage. During the battle of Surigao Straits, a large piece of shrapnel fell on my boat from an explosion directed at airplanes high overhead. Fortunately, PT-138 was in dry dock at the time, having repairs made to the bottom. With so much metal thrown into the sky above us, falling shrapnel was an existential threat. While at Tacloban, we were granted permission to come alongside a cruiser to take custody of the body of an army captain killed by falling shrapnel as he was boarding the ship.

The weather in the Philippines was usually good while I was there. However, in late 1944, a hurricane gusted in from the southeast. PT boats were all moved out into the bay to avoid being pushed onto shore or into each other. Wind speed continued to build. We anchored with very heavy line and waited for the squall. It arrived in the early evening. Great gusts of wind and water assaulted the boat. We could make out lights passing us in the night, ships being blown about. The tension on the bow anchor line became so strong that we began to drag the anchor, putting PT-138 and other vessels at risk in the crowded harbor. With that much tension, it would be impossible to bring the anchor on deck. I took a crewman with me to the bow. Holding tight to the lifeline, I used an ax to cut the line, then turned the boat in the direction of the docks in search of calmer water, somewhere better safeguarded from the wind. We spotted a large freighter with blazing deck lights and, beyond it, the docks. Securing the boat to the docks with tension lines and mooring snubbers, we got some sleep. Morning came, and we went out into the bay to survey the damage from the previous night. The shore was littered with small boats, and one PT had been thrown onto the beach.

The crews of PT-138 and PT-137 were frequently partnered on night patrols and during the day. With our bows pushed up onto the sand of a small island on the Samar side of the bay with Leyte, we were enjoying the tranquility of the secluded beach when the sound of a small plane engine breached the quiet, followed by the whine of a bomb falling, then another. The plane appeared no larger than a Cessna, and the pilot was targeting our stationary boats. Both shells landed about one hundred yards away. The Japanese were down to students fresh from flight training.

Ensign Smith (center/front row) and the crew
of PT-138 at Tacloban or Ormoc Bay.

The war continued. It was after April 12, 1945. On Samar, across from Tacloban, the US Navy Construction Battalion ("Seabees") built a campsite for us with tents for sleeping, an officer's mess hall, and a Quonset hut to be used as an officer's club. A cot in one of the tents was mine, and I sometimes got some sleep there. The tender in the harbor carried supplies for all the PT boats in the area and served as our headquarters. I stood at the dock, awaiting the boat that would take me to the tender. When it arrived, a friend stepped from the boat. "President Roosevelt is dead," he pronounced. FDR had been president for nearly half of my life, and the news saddened me. It all seemed so far away.

Tacloban had become too far removed from action with the Japanese and the squadron was moved from Tacloban on the east coast of Leyte to Ormoc Bay on the western side. Ormoc was a small village with a smattering of small Filipino houses. The remains of two large ships broke the surface of the water, doubtless the victims of earlier attacks. A good dock extended out into the bay, and a swift stream came down from the hills. Filipino women were seen beating clothes on rocks in the stream and drying them in the sun. It was rough treatment, and I had them clean my T-shirts and shorts only once.

The move to Ormoc was to facilitate the patrol of Cebu, an island to the west that remained in Japanese hands. Our night patrols were south along the Cebu coastline, usually stopping short of Cebu City. We encountered little barge activity until we took a longer patrol down the entire east coast of the island, keeping a mile or so offshore. In the middle of the night, radar detected a ship on a course from Mindanao north to Cebu City. Estimating the ship was a mile away, we pushed our speed up to twenty-five knots and set a course to intercept the ship. The sky was clear, the moon was bright, and the illuminated ship was exposed. Our boats fell into line for a run on the starboard side. All guns opened fire at a distance of fifty to one hundred yards. After the first run, a second was not necessary. The small cargo ship was on fire, and people were making their escapes. The waters were calm, and the Japanese sailors had plenty of time to get into boats and make their way to the nearby shore. We made no effort at rescue.

Returning to base on a course to the northeast, we opted to run up the coast of Bohol, the Mactan Island of Cebu, on our port side. A few hundred yards ashore, bathed in the moonlight, I saw the outlines of the large statue of Portuguese explorer, Ferdinand Magellan, who arrived there in 1521. To honor him, it was erected by the colonizing Portuguese 345 years after Magellan died at the hands of the Mactan natives of the island.

We had a good night and, on returning to base, learned that the navy public relations office knew about it and wanted to do a story. A photographer took pictures of the crew, and the exaggerated story appeared in the *Knoxville Journal*, along with a picture of me in the cockpit, the bulkhead showing clear signs of having taken enemy fire. I never would have been at the helm without my helmet on. The article was clipped and pasted into the scrapbooks of my mother and sisters back home.

The Philippines is an archipelago of about 7,100 islands. Though we expected a push north into Luzon, for now it was quiet. I was ordered to rotate back to the States for leave, marking the end of my year in the South Pacific. Commodore Harlee, the executive officer for all PT operations in the Pacific and the only commodore on active duty, was also returning to the States. The idea for a farewell party for the commodore was born. I ran the idea up the chain of command. They agreed. We found a few gallons of colorless 180-

proof grain alcohol used in our torpedoes motors and hid them for the party to be convened in the recently constructed office's mess hall on Samar. Army nurses from Tacloban were invited, and the party was set to kickoff at 6:30 p.m.

By 5:00 p.m. that afternoon, the alcohol had been delivered to the kitchen, the mess hall crew had prepared the tables, and they were going about filling the water glasses. It was a simple mistake, but one that happened in nearly every glass. Mistaken for water, the alcohol now filled the water glasses. The error was discovered by an officer who set down his glass and wheezed, "This is not water!" We hastened to recover the glasses, which most of the officers refused to surrender, leaving our punch with less of a punch. All things considered, the party was a success. The nurses were entertained, the commodore went home with the love of his men, and the mission of the party conspirators was accomplished.

LEAVE IN THE STATES

March 10, 1945, I wrote to my parents. I was coming home. Transportation issues being what they were, I could only tell them to expect me in the spring, but before long, arrangements were made. A boat took me down the coast of Samar to a Seabee base at a small Filipino village on the coast. I waited for my flight. Having nothing else to do, the base commander appointed me officer of the day, every day, with the duty of standing at the entrance to the base and the village, checking everyone entering. Generally, the visitors were the village school teachers and children, and each morning, I would engage them in conversation. They were a happy bunch. They smiled, and one offered me marital advice. I should marry a Filipino woman. "Americans that marry Filipino women always get rich."

There were few signs that the Japanese had any interest in moving into Samar. It had little in the way of industry and no significant ports. The Ninety-Third Seabees, arriving only four months earlier, had built a significant airstrip near the village of Guiuan on the southernmost point of Samar that was capable of managing our largest planes. I borrowed a jeep from the Seabees and pointed it toward the small village I would reach at the end of a dirt road, shaded by dark foliage and palm trees encroaching on both sides. It was small, but it was the hub for the commerce of farmers and fishermen in the area. As I neared Guiuan, I came upon a small clearing and a group of about thirty people. I slowed to see what was going on. Clustered around a small ring, four posts with chicken wire stretched around them, they were betting on cockfighting; many of them clutching a gamecock to their sides, waiting for their bird's chance in the ring.

Leaving the cockfight behind, I continued on the unpaved road through thick tropical jungle, another two or three miles before arriving at my destination. Centrally located in Guiuan was an astonishing Catholic church I could not have expected in this remote village. It projected an opulence not reflected in the more primitive structures around it. The altar was heavily ornamented and stood before a wall covered in portraits of saints. Smaller shrines for prayer were set along the walls and windows. I was grateful for having made the trip and returned to the Seabee base with the jeep and a fond memory of that place.

After a week as officer of the day, I had a line on a plane headed to Hawaii. In the morning, I hurried to the airfield where P-39s were landing and taking off and found my place aboard a large four-engine transport, with thinly padded bucket seats along each side of the plane. The passengers arranged themselves as comfortably as possible for a very long flight. My luggage had been turned over to the flight crew before I boarded. It included a .27-caliber Japanese long rifle and ammunition. I had used it in sport shooting at flying fish as we returned from patrol. The fish had nothing to fear.

The plane's wheels lost contact with the runway, and the plane lifted into the brightening sky from Samar. There would be a few stops, but I was on my way home. Sometime in the early evening, we descended for a landing in Guam for refueling. Passengers descended the stairs to the tarmac for the brief chance to stretch. Over too soon, the break ended, and we climbed back aboard after midnight. The flight manifest of passengers, from seaman to commander and colonel, were spread throughout the cabin, settling in with no thought given to rank or seniority. Dawn broke, Hawaii was on the horizon, and we began our descent. I peered from a window and saw

a very small island ahead. The airstrip began at the water's edge on one side of the island and ended at the water's edge on the other side of the island. We were coming into Johnston Atoll, elevation: seven feet. During the war, it served as a refueling base for planes and submarines; one of the busiest air-transport terminals in the Pacific. It is about 750 miles west southwest of Hawaii and was acquired in 1858 as a minor outlying island territory of the United

States. Most of the island is taken up by the landing strip. We landed, refueled, and again ascended, destination: Honolulu. It had been a long night in the air, sometimes in rough weather. I was sleep deprived, but excited.

We touched down and taxied to the terminal. There, we collected our luggage; in my case, minus my Japanese rifle. The plane crew disavowed any knowledge of it, and I never saw it again. A navy bus arrived and took us to our quarters for the evening, mine in a bachelor officer quarters. Food and shelter handled, our immediate task was to find transportation to San Francisco. My navy travel companions and I preferred getting a flight, but despite five days of maneuvering to get seats, we finally settled on a US-leased Australian passenger ship to get us home. Once I was settled into my state room and had selected my meal service, getting home on a luxury liner was looking pretty good. In fact, I could get used to being treated like a private passenger over the next five days. Early one morning, I awoke to see California on the horizon, appearing to rise from the ocean, and in short order, we were passing under the Golden Gate Bridge. With some sentiment, I recalled my thoughts as I passed under the bridge a year earlier in the other direction. I thought of PT-138 and the buddies I had left behind. Our ship steamed into the harbor and docked. A sailing schedule would have invited the attack of enemy warships, so one was not published. "Loose lips sink ships." Nevertheless, throngs waited at the dock for our arrival. Leaving the ship with my baggage in tow, I hailed a taxi to the centrally located Saint Francis Hotel at Union Square, where Shreve and other shipmates were staying, having arrived ahead of me.

Promoted from ensign to lieutenant junior grade (Lt. JG) some months earlier, I had not yet found the proper insignia for my uniform. An officer, who had been promoted to lieutenant noticed and handed me his half stripe. A seamstress at a nearby dry cleaner quickly stitched it to the sleeve of my jacket. The tropics left me in need of a general cleanup. I found a barber shop to fulfill a long held whim, a professional haircut, and shave. It would be the first and last time someone else gave me a shave. My third priority took me back to the dry cleaner with all my uniforms. Other than while on leave in

Sydney, they had not been worn in the past year. I had them pressed while I waited behind a curtain in my skivvies.

Union Square has always been celebrated for its retail shopping, fine dining, and nightlife. That evening, I joined my friends and went out on the town. While that might conjure images of drunken sailors holding each other up; it was rather restrained. Simply being able to walk into a nice restaurant and order a fine meal was a great departure from our lives in the tropics. There were parties at various venues in the city, but my attention was on finding transportation across the country. San Francisco was fun, but my priority was walking into the home of my parents at Walnut Hill. A plane would get me there in one or two days. A train would require five days. In the morning, I explored the flying option. I know they had worried about their son at war in the South Pacific and had prayed a thousand prayers, so on arrival in San Francisco, I let Mom know I had made it that far.

Commercial airlines in 1945 were not as prevalent as today. Nor were there jetliners flying coast to coast. I secured a seat aboard an Eastern Airlines C-47 leaving in two days. That night, Ed McNamara and I went out. He was bringing my Colt .45 back for me, carrying a lighter bag. Ed was from the Boston area and lived a storied life. He played football on an athletic scholarship to Holy Cross and was taken by the New York Giants in the twenty-seventh round of the 1943 NFL draft before joining the navy. He was the skipper of PT-127 and was awarded the Silver Star for courageous action under fire. After the war, he returned to football briefly before joining the FBI and serving as a principal investigator of the Brinks Robbery in 1950. Following a gambling scandal involving the Boston police commissioner, Ed was appointed to the position at a volatile time in Boston that included the murders of thirteen women by the Boston Strangler. He was the first career law enforcement officer appointed to the job in the twentieth century. I never saw my Colt .45 again.

I was at the airport early the next morning. Refueling stops in Phoenix, Dallas, and Nashville made for a long day and night. In stormy weather, the flight from Nashville to Knoxville shuddered and bounced around in the sky, and I will confess to wondering if I had survived the war only to end up in the rubble of a plane crash in my home state. As night became day, we arrived in Knoxville, and an airport bus brought us into the city. At the Greyhound Bus Station, I purchased a ticket for Harriman. The trip was about forty-five miles, through the small Tennessee towns of Clinton, the edge of Oak Ridge, and to Oliver Springs before the last dozen miles to Harriman. During wartime rationing, commercial transportation survived by resourcefulness and whatever equipment was available to keep engines in good repair and operational. This was no less true of the Greyhound that had so far gotten through Oliver Springs and to about a half mile from Walnut Hill before the engine sputtered and coughed before going silent, leaving me to consider grabbing my bag and walking the last stretch. The decision was made for me when after another half an hour, the driver returned to his seat and brought the engine to life again. I had moved from my seat to the door well, and the driver stopped in front of the house. Grabbing my bags, I walked to the house to be warmly greeted by my mother's long embrace.

It was a thirty-day leave. I relaxed at home, sometimes going in to town and seeking old friends. Most were away, involved in the war effort. I got a taste of rationing rules under which America had been operating while I was away. The lives of my parents were unchanged. Ona and Glenna were in school at LMU. Wallace was in Florida, training with the air force; and Vee and Oba lived nearby. Two bottles of bourbon were kept in my locked suitcase, knowing that I would be disowned if Mom found them. So when Jean was showing signs of the flu and had difficulty sleeping, I prepared a "hot toddy" for her and quietly claimed credit when she got the sleep she was missing and was well again.

I attended Walnut Hill Baptist Church with my parents during my leave. After one service, I was approached by Dave Christmas, a longtime resident of the area. He asked about his son, JD Christmas, who followed me in school by a handful of years. JD served on the crew of a navy plane and had been reported missing after his plane went down in the Pacific. Dave was hopeful that I could share something that might suggest his son could have survived. I had seen planes go down like that. I could not pretend optimism. I wished I could.

In Oak Ridge, I visited with my old roommate, Gorman Hill; his sister, Jennie; his brother; and his mother. Then Gorman and I went over to the home of Bill and Mary Ruth Covey, also classmates at LMU. Gorman and Bill were both employed in the nuclear program at Oak Ridge, where I had worked briefly before active duty. My curiosity then never satisfied, I asked what they were building, and Covey answered, "Doug, they are producing something so powerful they don't know if they can control it." I was in Cuba when the bombs were dropped on Hiroshima and Nagasaki, and I understood then what Covey had told me.

GUANTANOMO BAY, CUBA

Thirty days of leave had passed, and I had orders to report to the motor torpedo boat training base in Melville, Rhode Island. Flagging down a Greyhound bus in front of the house, I rode to Knoxville, catching the train for Washington, D.C., New York, and Providence. After a year of active duty overseas, returning officers were expected to assist in the instructional program for a month or two before another tour of duty in the South Pacific. We were all convinced that the next tour would take us all the way to Japan. Experience had taught us the Japanese would fight to the end, and we expected patrolling there to be especially hazardous. But for now, life for returning officers in Melville was easy. On my second day back, I was the officer of the day, mustering the men early in the morning and reading the orders of the day to the assembled officers. When the men stood at attention, I approached the microphone in a small nearby office, turned it on, and began to read the orders; none of it very interesting until I got to this one. Four PTs would be immediately dispatched to the naval facility at Guantanamo Bay, Cuba, to assist in the shakedown operations of new US Cruisers, ships to be used in the invasion of Japan. The role of the PTs was to simulate the nighttime attacks of the Japanese suicide torpedo boats.

Interested parties were invited into the office to sign up. I thought of Cuba as another tropical paradise, but without the Japanese shooting at me. Mine was the first name on the list. In two days, four boats were fueled and provisioned for the trip down the east coast. Beyond our responsibilities of supervising activities of the boat, each officer was assigned additional duties for the success of the mission. I assume it was randomly decided that I would be the supply officer, tasked with finding ship supply ashore and replenishing the boats. Assigned to PT-452 of Squadron 4, crews of the four boats cast off their lines from the Melville docks and set out through Narragansett Bay and into the Atlantic. Cruising west southwest, we entered Long Island Sound and arrived at navy docks in Brooklyn for the night. The next day, we proceeded down the East River, into New York harbor, and again out into the Atlantic Ocean. We were headed southward down the east coast, turning up the Delaware River, to the navy shipyard at Philadelphia.

Nine officers and twenty-three enlisted men comprised our collective crew. A lieutenant named Chris was in command. Other officers on this adventure included Jim from Georgia, and Bob Geddings, the other officer on my boat who called Philadelphia home. His family owned a shoe-manufacturing business. He had arranged dates for us. Dinner and dancing were followed by conversation at the home of Bob's girlfriend, impressing the girls and the girlfriend's father with our exploits at sea. At one point, I launched into the history of an old navy ship in the Hudson Bay near Columbia University, unaware that the girlfriend's father was a retired navy captain, who doubtlessly knew far more about it than I did.

We put out into the Atlantic, generally four or five miles off the coastline, going south at twenty knots with a planned overnight stay at the naval base in Norfolk, Virginia. One of my old squadron commanders from Ormoc Bay was there, and we did some catching up with each other. We did not carry much in the way of provisions accounting for the frequent stops. We continued on our southern tour of the east coast with stops in Beaufort, North Carolina; Jacksonville, Florida; and Miami, Florida, where we refueled, reprovisioned, and killed time for four days before setting out for Nuevitas, Cuba, on our way to Guantanamo Bay.

We brought our boats into Biscayne Bay and downtown Miami. Prior to docking, my friend Jim from Georgia assured me that his cousin, who worked at Eastern Airlines, was the girl for me, and he was going to make the introductions. We tied up to the dock. Jim disappeared, and the crews of the four boats scattered. We expected to be there for two days. There were numerous parties. I met a girl from South Carolina, whose last name was Lyles. She became my date for dinner, dancing, swimming at the beach, and visiting many of the nightspots Miami had to offer. In the course of our time together, I learned that she was Mrs. Lyles. Her husband, an air force officer, had recently been killed in action. I never saw or heard from her again.

The weather turned to a sloppy, wind-driven rain, and Chris suspended our advance on Cuba for a day, and one day became two. Jim was rarely around, but he did finally introduce me to his cousin. However, it quickly became apparent that Jim himself had fallen for his cousin, and he no longer thought she was the girl for me. My suspicions were later confirmed. In the summer of 1946, I had been discharged from the navy and was home, waiting for the fall term to begin at the University of Michigan. In our yard, I was playing touch football with some of the local kids when a car stopped. Jim and his "cousin" got out. Recently married, they were on their honeymoon. She showed me her ring, and we all got a good laugh at Jim's promise to fix me up with his cousin.

The weather cleared, and we pushed on to Nuevitas and further south to Guantanamo Bay. I lived in the barracks for navy officers and took my meals at the officer's mess. The barracks was a one-story plain-wooden structure. In a large room with eight other officers, I slept comfortably on a cot. On the southern facing side of Cuba's eastern tip, the base was bounded by the bay, the Caribbean, and the mountains of southeastern Cuba. Free bus service was available. It was easy duty.

Two or three nights of each week, we were ordered out to sea to carry out our mock attacks on the new cruisers. Our days were free. We attempted golf on sandy fairways and greens. The bus frequently

OFFICERS' MESS
NAVAL OPERATING BASE,
GUANTANAMO BAY, CUBA

W. D. Smith

is registered as a member of the
Officers' Mess for the year ending December 31, 194 5

C. G. Malburn
Manager

took me to the library to check out a book. On off nights, we met at the officer's club for drinks and conversation, or we could go to an

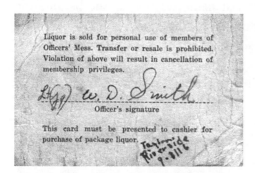

outdoor movie. A superior Cuban made cigar could be had for just a few cents. I often sat on a stool out-doors watching a movie and pulling on a cigar.

Navy Day was first celebrated on October 27, 1922, and when the date rolled around in the autumn of 1945, I was on one of the two PT boats sent to Palm Beach for public display. People came aboard and the crewmen, in their dress whites, enjoyed the attention. Two days in Palm Beach behind us, we again pointed the boats in the direction of Nuevitas on the north coast of Cuba for refueling and an overnight in the harbor on our way back to Guantanamo. Contrary to intentions, we were there for five days.

Nuevitas is a small coastal town, some two hundred miles from Guantanamo. We found the narrow entrance to the harbor in the late afternoon, leading us to the village of Nuevitas on the banks of a large bay, consisting of a few buildings and a dock in the distance. We first refueled at a shipping dock located at the end of a railroad track coming from the village. We had only just tied up, when we saw a lone figure coming up the track from the village with a heavy sack on his back. Reaching us, we saw that he was a middle-aged Black man. He gently lowered the sack to the ground and inquired with a heavy British accent, "Would you fellows like to buy a cold coke?" His sack was filled with them.

Of my wartime memories, Nuevitas remains one of the best. The entire town would come out to the square at night. The girls would promenade in one direction and the boys in the other, around and around the square. Older women chaperones sat in the shade and watched their young charges. On weekends, and sometimes more often, a band played from a pavilion in the park and the town; old and young welcomed us when we joined them in Cuban dances.

Again, the weather turned bad. Chris had delayed our departure for Guantanamo a day at a time until we had been there five days. On our return to the base, we had taken on two days of supplies in Miami, which were exhausted by the extra three days in Nuevitas. More provisions were acquired in Nuevitas at the ship's chandler. My shopping list included meat, vegetables, and other items, including penicillin for the less-discriminating seamen who had contracted a venereal disease in Florida. Finally, the base commander ordered us to his base, regardless of the weather. We left that night. For the next three hours, our boats were violently tossed about in my worst ever three hours at sea.

When the war in Europe came to an end with an unconditional surrender of the Axis powers on May 8, 1945, Victory in Europe Day (VE Day), the combatants could exhale, and the celebration began, including in Guantanamo. The navy base hosted a big dance. Pretty Cuban girls were brought over from Santiago de Cuba, fifty miles to the west. The women wearing long formal dresses; navy officers in dress-white uniforms spun them around the dance floor to a variety of music until late into the night.

A few weeks later, two of our PT boats cruised over to Santiago to tour the town that, since its establishment in the 1500s by the Spanish, has been dominated by an old fort standing at the edge of the harbor. The town is known for its colonial architecture and, in the 1950s, would become the place from which a highly organized urban resistance to the government would launch. Fidel Castro would proclaim the Cuban Revolution victorious from the balcony of the Santiago de Cuba City Hall.

Our return trip was in rough seas. The crew had adopted a mixed-breed dog in Palm Beach. The dog should have been secured below deck in that kind of weather but apparently fell overboard unnoticed, saddening the crew after a good day at Santiago.

Contemporaneous with our celebrating VE Day in Cuba, the Allies were anxious to also close the book on the war in the Pacific. Cloaked in secrecy since its beginnings in Oak Ridge, where I had worked for three months before activation, the component parts of the first atomic bomb were crated and shipped to San Francisco where the parts became cargo on the USS Indianapolis. In mid-July 1945, the Portland-class heavy cruiser, once based in Pearl Harbor and once successfully targeted by a kamikaze, passed under the Golden Gate Bridge and raced to a US air base on Tinian, part of the Marianas Islands, 1,570 miles from Hiroshima. After only ten days at sea, the delivery was made on July 26, 1945. The stealth mission remained so as the Indianapolis departed Tinian, ultimately bound for Leyte Gulf. About halfway there, two Japanese torpedoes launched from a submarine and detonated, sinking the Indianapolis in twelve minutes. When the ship failed to arrive in Leyte as scheduled on July 31, it was not reported missing. Of the 1,200 men on board, 316 survived the sinking, their injuries, and the sharks. They were discovered by accident on August 2, 1945. The tragedy was not disclosed by the government until August 15, 1945, the same day it announced Japan's surrender.

Hiroshima and Nagasaki are the two cities being synonymous with the pivotal moment that brought Japan to its knees, bringing the war in the Pacific to a climatic end. The expectation that our next patrol duty would be along the Japanese coast was undone. Japan surrendered, and the war was over. Abruptly, we would be returning to our civilian lives.

Anticipated orders were issued directing us to bring the four PT boats back up the Atlantic Coast to the Brooklyn Navy Yard for salvage and decommissioning, retiring them from service to the armed forces at the end of their useful lives. PT-boat duty was perilous, and the squadrons had suffered high losses. Of the 531 PT boats serving during World War II in the Pacific, the Mediterranean, the Aleutian Islands of Alaska after the Japanese Army landed there, and in the English Channel, upwards of 432 would survive to be decommissioned. We had lost 18.6 percent of the PT fleet, either sunk or otherwise lost to other causes. PT boats had served multiple purposes—harassing enemy shore installations, supporting friendly troop landings, destroying floating mines, sinking enemy shipping targets, destroying enemy landing barges, rescuing downed pilots, landing partisans behind enemy lines, and attacking enemy island outposts—but without a war, their services were no longer needed.

XVILLE JOURNAL
September 30, 1945

WINS NAVY CITATION—Lt. (jg) Walter D. Smith, 27, USNR, left, whose parents, Mr. and Mrs. Walter B. Smith, live at Harriman, Route 2, is congratulated by Commodore J. J. Mahoney, USN, commanding officer of the Naval operating base, Guantanamo Bay, Cuba, after receiving the Navy Unit Commendation Ribbon for participating in naval operations with the Seventh Fleet's Motor Torpedo Squadron Seven in the Pacific.

The war was over, and we would all soon be civilians. The burden of future combat was no longer a cloud over our lives. With the war over, the armed forces had thousands of young men to discharge from service and the defense department payroll.

Our trip north in December of 1945 was a lark. Reaching Jacksonville, Florida, the sea was choppy with waves cresting in whitecaps. We tucked into the Intracoastal Waterway and easily and safely made way from Jacksonville all the way to Norfolk, Virginia. Memorably, on the Georgia leg, my boat ran aground. Running the boat in reverse did not free us from the sandbar. Another boat attached a towline and another passed by at high speed to create a wave to lift my boat. It succeeded, and we were liberated from the hidden menace.

In 1942, the German Afrika Korps was poorly supported by the Nazi's and found itself squeezed between the Americans to the West and the British to the East. By May 1943, the allies contended with 275,000 German and Italian prisoners, a logistical nightmare at the end of an already overburdened supply line. A clever answer was found. Otherwise returning empty, the liberty ships in the Mediterranean, at great risk of attack by German submarines, were used to transport the prisoners to the United States. The general knowledge that German soldiers were on those ships may have kept them safe.

Going north, the Intracoastal Waterway leaves the Stono River in the low country of South Carolina, emerging in Charleston Harbor. Our passage treated us to a spectacle of beautiful scenery, antebellum mansions steeped in elegance, grace and history dotting the banks, quaint-fishing marinas, stores and restaurants, and wildlife that inhabited the Waterway—including the occasional dolphin, pelicans, and osprey. Less than half a mile across the harbor on the western side of the peninsula, we found the coast guard docks and tied up, not far from the Medical University of South Carolina. As we stepped away from the docks, I saw German prisoners of war in prison garb, working at various menial jobs. I later learned that they had been sent to work on farms in Florence County and many other places in South Carolina and the South generally. Although there were prisoners of war in many states, they were concentrated in the South due to climate considerations for year-round housing. There was an obvious shortage of male laborers during the war, and those POW's who labored on farms were invaluable. After the war, some stayed and became citizens.

Charleston in 1945 was not the Charleston of today. We took the opportunity to stretch our legs with a stroll through the streets of Charleston, and finding little activity of interest, we made our way back to the docks. We continued our way north on the Intracoastal Waterway, traversing bays, rivers, and canals in North Carolina, finally stopping at the docks in Elizabeth City, North Carolina. The locals came out to see the boats and to chat with us about the boats and the war. A local doctor took several of us to his home for dinner that night. Going out of my way in 1996, I returned to see Elizabeth City again, finding it remains a small town on the Intracoastal Waterway with a rich maritime history.

We had enjoyed better than expected weather for December. That ended at our next stop in Norfolk, Virginia. The thermometer dropped fifty degrees, and thereafter, we went about our work in cold weather gear. In the morning, we left Norfolk behind and turned out into the Atlantic, with a plan of completing the balance of our trip that day. It was cold and dark when we saw the first buoy outside of the harbor in New York, not our target, but there were more miles behind us than ahead. That first buoy is still a long way from the Brooklyn Navy Yard, but we finally arrived, tied up the boats, and climbed into cold bunks. Christmas was near, and the base was all but deserted. We were given Christmas leave the next day, and I was on a train to Tennessee.

The trip took me through the capital in Washington, and I visited the Navy Annex to the PT boat desk to inquire about my next assignment. There I found Commander David Olds. He had been our squadron exec during much of my assignment to the South Pacific. I asked for an assignment to navy flight training and learned that no new people were being accepted. There were two Naval Reserve Officer Training Corp (NROTC) positions available at Brown University and at the University of Michigan. I opted for Michigan. Dave cut my orders for Ann Arbor, and I continued on to Harriman for Christmas (1945). The cloud of war removed, President Truman had declared a four-day holiday for federal employees.

ANN ARBOR

Captain Michaux directed the NROTC program at Michigan, and I reported to him the following January. Of medium build with a narrow-gray mustache, he was always formal in his relations with the staff. I later learned that he had served as the navy base commander in Sydney and had signed my leave orders when I left, unaware I was destined for the battle of Leyte Gulf.

The weather in Ann Arbor was not an improvement from the weather I had experienced during my active duty days in Rhode Island or New York. Each morning, bundled in my heavy navy coat, ear muffs, scarf, gloves, and usually rubber overshoes, I walked from my room in the Michigan Union on the West Quad to the NROTC building a few blocks away. The three-storied building housed the navy teaching staff and classrooms. My NROTC assignment was to be in charge of all audio/visual teaching aids, about which I knew nothing, and I was to teach courses in seamanship and fire control. I had very real experience in both. I soon learned how to dismantle, repair, and reassemble all the various projectors that were used, and I maintained the collection of films and slides used in the classes. My job was made more difficult by my predecessors, who had cataloged none of the equipment, film, or slides. With little else to do, the cataloging became my priority. My teaching was frequently informed by experience or what I had learned on my own the night before. The university listed me as "assistant professor of Naval Science and Tactics." My orders indicated that I carried that title "without pay" by the university.

ED/
9 Serial 311065 (fjb)   HEADQUARTERS
       32-30339-46   NINTH NAVAL DISTRICT
                                GREAT LAKES, ILLINOIS

                              18 June 1946

From: Commandant, NINTH Naval District.   NAVAL R.O.T.C. UNIT
To: Lieut. (jg) Walter Douglas SMITH, (D),
         University of Michigan
         Naval Reserve Officers Training Corps   JUN 20 1946
         Ann Arbor Michigan
                                                  RECEIVED
                                                  UNIVERSITY OF MICHIGAN
Via: PNS&T University of Michigan

Subj: Release to inactive duty.

Refs: (a) P16-3/00 (D620) dtd 15 June 1946

         (b) ALNAV 161-46

1.   Pursuant to reference (a), when directed by your commanding officer,
you will consider yourself detached from your present duty and from
such other duties as may have been assigned, in time to proceed immediately to:

         Commanding Officer
         Officer Separation Center
         Great Lakes Illinois
and report to the commanding officer on   10 July 1946
for temporary duty pending release to inactive duty in accordance with the
provisions of reference (b).

2.   Upon completion of this temporary duty, you will, when directed, regard
yourself detached and proceed to your home for release from active duty in
accordance with instructions to be issued by the commanding officer.

                                                  G. D. MURRAY.

A "captain's mast" is a nonjudicial procedure for the command to address minor infractions. An NROTC student had been charged with being "absent without leave" (AWOL), and I was appointed to represent him in the hearing, introducing evidence and questioning witnesses, presenting the boy's case as best I could, but once it was established that he was voluntarily absent, only one question remained: Was he was given leave? It did not go well for him. Captain Michaux dismissed him from NROTC, and the student was immediately shipped to the Great Lakes training station near Chicago, where he became an ordinary seaman, going through basic training. The navy could not tolerate sailors going absent without leave.

My association with the NROTC program was limited to the spring of 1946 and included an order to install a six-inch navy cannon turret atop the portico at the entrance to the building. It became my job because the cannon had been classified as a visual aid. That seemed like a stretch then and now, but as it turned out, my involvement was to handle the paperwork and to supervise the project, another job for which I was not really qualified. One day, a large truck and crane appeared with the gun. Experts were on hand to shore up the supporting columns. I expect that the gun, the visual aid, is still there today.

As the NROTC spring began, I was looking over the university's spring-course schedule. I had enjoyed psychology as it was taught by Dr. Jess Edds at LMU and decided to enroll in a course. "Child Growth and Behavior" was a three-hour credit, taught on Saturdays by Dr. Willard Olson.

He was a professor of psychology and education, with a doctoral degree from the University of Minnesota, studying under Dr. John Anderson, a well-known and respected researcher in the psychology field of child development. I enrolled; my first step toward a graduate degree in a program I found intriguing.

I was released from the navy in the summer of 1946 and remained at the University until 1950. The release procedure required a day or so in Chicago, and at the end of the process, my active duty commitment was fulfilled, but I remained in the Navy Reserve and maintained that relationship with the navy for the next dozen years. I left Chicago and spent a few days in Harriman before becoming a full-time graduate student in educational psychology, initially pursuing a master's degree. A tall fellow with reddish hair named Dr. Clark Trow was my advisor. He had authored a few books, played the viola in the University Orchestra, and occupied a respected position in Ann Arbor's academic community.

As the navy residential program was being discontinued, the university was facing an influx of GI-Bill students who had put off their futures to serve their country. It needed staff to manage the various programs associated with operating its facilities, housing several hundred undergraduates in two large residence halls, East and West

Quadrangles. Having lived in the West Quad while teaching, I was familiar with the director and was given the job of director of men's intramural athletics. In exchange for a stipend, free room and free board, I prepared intramural game schedules and made certain that sports equipment was available. Importantly, I identified a sufficient number of student assistants to keep the program active. The pay covered my expenses, and GI-Bill money covered my educational expenses. Life was good and about to get better.

RHONDDA

The fall semester of 1946 kept me very busy. My course work was progressing well, and the intramural sports program was humming along. I enjoyed living in the dorm with the undergraduate students. Christmas was nearing when I read an ad in the campus paper. It was soliciting riders going south toward Atlanta for the holidays to share in the travel expenses. I answered the ad and soon found myself on the way to Harriman with the student owning the car and another passenger. We drove through the night across Ohio and Kentucky. Late in the night, we heard on the radio that Georgia's governor, Talmadge, who had only just been elected to a fourth term in the preceding November, died before his inauguration. The Georgia boy offered his condolences. "Thank God."

On my second day in Harriman, a Christmas card from Rhondda Miller arrived. She was visiting people in Bradenton, Florida. I fondly remembered our twenty-eight-day date in Sydney; I called a florist and sent her a dozen red roses with an invitation to visit Harriman. In a few days, I received her reply. She was on her way. Since receiving her card, my mind was consumed by the thought of seeing her again. Just after Christmas of 1946, her long bus ride from south of Tampa, through Georgia and Tennessee, had delivered her to Knoxville where I was waiting. Moving her luggage to another bus, we boarded for her last forty miles to Harriman. We had not seen each other in more than two years, though we had exchanged a few letters. Within the first few minutes of seeing her again, I proposed marriage...on a Greyhound bus. Without hesitation, she answered yes. Within the hour, she met Mom and Dad for the first time. I suppose we could have given it more thought, been less impulsive, but after a fifty-two-year marriage, I am prepared to say it was a success.

When the holiday came to an end, Rhondda joined me in the backseat of the Georgia boy's car for our return to Ann Arbor. I can only imagine the kitchen-table conversation we left behind. She stayed a day or two at the student union before leaving for Columbus, Indiana, to visit her sister Joyce and her sister's husband, David Compton. The wedding was scheduled for April 5, 1947 at the parsonage of a Baptist minister in Ann Arbor. It was the first day of spring break at the university. Joyce had arrived in Detroit the previous day. There were glitches in our plans to overcome. Rhondda's clothes had not arrived, so the girls went shopping for a dress. Beginning the night before our wedding, a heavy rain fell. Busses and trains were not running. My best man and undergraduate friend, Jim Baird, drove his father's car the fifty miles to Detroit to bring Rhondda and Joyce to the wedding.

Our guests included Joe Izzo, who served in the NROTC program with me; Maria, a graduate student from Montevideo, Uruguay; Jim Dorland from Saginaw; and Henry Godt of Fort Smith, Arkansas. The wedding party followed the ceremony with dinner in a Detroit restaurant. For the first time, Rhondda used her married name when she ordered a drink, signing a form to certify she was over twenty-one years old. In 1947, Gatlinburg had only two nice hotels and a couple of restaurants to offer us on our honeymoon. After a few days there, we went on to Harriman, eighty to a hundred miles west. Rhondda stayed there while I returned to Ann Arbor to find an apartment. It was not until June that I was successful. Frances and Bob Wirtz agreed to sublet their apartment for the summer, and Rhondda joined me in Ann Arbor. She found a job at the West Quadrangle post office, working with two young women who became her friends. I was invited by Dr. Olson to be his graduate assistant. Throw in the GI-Bill money, and by the end of summer 1947, we were set financially, at least our monthly income exceeded our debt. However, the end of our lease was looming, and finding another place was proving more difficult than expected.

Ultimately, we came upon an ad in the campus paper seeking a married couple to share an apartment with an elderly gentleman. We answered the ad. Mr. Bohr occupied a downstairs duplex apartment, with five rooms and one bath. He had retired from the US Consular Service, working in a US embassy. Rather short, Mr. Bohr was about seventy-five years old, quiet, and surprisingly strong and active. His son David was a professor at the medical school. Rhondda and I were to provide the meals. No money would be exchanged. It was intended to be a short-term fix, though the arrangement lasted a year and became increasingly dissatisfactory. Rhondda had not bargained for cleaning after two men. It bothered me less. Mr. Bohr was a fine old gentleman who tolerated us in his home. He and I tended a vegetable garden behind the house together for so long as we were in Ann Arbor, and we became friends with the young couple who took our place in the duplex.

Ray Scott was an assistant professor in engineering, who lived with his wife, Dorothy, in an upstairs apartment. When they built a house and packed the moving van, we took over the apartment, and Rhondda was happy. She was happier still when in 1948, her parents, Henry and Lyn, were allowed to immigrate to the United States in a convoluted route from Australia to South Africa, then to Windsor, Ontario, just across the river from Detroit. They waited there until their tickets were punched to enter the country in a period of months. Expecting to be cleared to cross the river soon, Mr. Miller gave me money to buy a car for him. He liked Chryslers, and with his approval, Rhondda and I bought a four-door Chrysler. On weekends, we crossed the Ambassador Bridge over the Detroit River to Windsor and their apartment, and he would take the opportunity to drive his car. Of course, as we say of the UK, Australians drive on the "wrong" side of the road, and the steering wheel in front of the passenger seat took some adjustment. At the end of our visit, Mrs. Miller would load the car with groceries for us, clothes for Rhondda, and frequently furs and other items for their future home in the States. They remained in Windsor four or five months before everything was in order for their entry, and we reluctantly surrendered the Chrysler. Conveniently, it was during this time that a large shipping crate from Sydney reached the docks in Detroit. It measured at least eight feet by ten feet by sixteen feet, requiring a large crane to lift it. An engineer, Mr. Miller had designed and built the crate himself because that is the kind of guy he was. It was loaded with the furniture they wanted in their new home. We rented a large four-wheel trailer in Ann Arbor, and with Mr. Miller, we drove to Detroit to bring the furniture back in at least three trips. They were large heavy pieces that we struggled to lift and load onto the trailer. It was all brought back to our apartment for storage and use until the Millers were ready for it. The place was stuffed with furniture, with narrow pathways to get from room to room. That furniture is now distributed among their grandchildren for the most part.

The Millers left Ann Arbor for Santa Cruz, California, bought a yard and outdoor furniture store, and worked it for a few years. It was in the early fifties that Rhondda's brother, Ian, successfully negotiated with US Immigration to allow him to join his parents and sisters in this country. As required by immigration laws, he was considered a person with special skills (architecture). He entered the University of California at Berkeley and completed his master's degree in architecture. Rhondda became a US citizen while in Ann Arbor, and along the way, Ian, Joyce, and their parents also became naturalized citizens. Ian took a job with a firm in San Francisco, designing some of the tall buildings downtown, before joining a firm in Seattle, where he met the Canadian he would later marry, Donna.

I began my work as Dr. Olson's graduate assistant in the large lecture section, delivering the lecture if he had to be away. His work with children was imaginative, and the respect he enjoyed on campus was well earned. His textbook on "child growth and behavior" was widely adopted. He turned me loose to find my topic for doctoral research and invited me to consult with him as needed. My work with Dr. Olson lasted three years. He was a fine boss, and we corresponded on occasion, even after my arrival at Florida State years later.

During those first years of marriage, 1947 to 1949, I worked and studied. Rhondda continued at the post office. We enjoyed living in Ann Arbor. Well-known authors and researchers from around the country delivered their lectures, and we were excited to be in attendance. Bicycles provided our transportation. The university did not permit students to bring automobiles on campus. Baskets were affixed to the bicycles, allowing us to haul books, groceries, and other items. Everyone got around on bikes, students, staff, and faculty. They were everywhere. Rhondda, however, had never learned to ride a bike. We went to the playground of a nearby school, where I taught my twenty-seven-year-old wife to do what her future children would learn by age five. After a few falls and some salty venting born out of frustration, she learned.

Movies were a regular Saturday night date for us as well as many other graduate students. Then, there was Michigan football, and we had season tickets. The Wolverines were undefeated in back-to-back seasons, 1947 and 1948, winning the national championship in 1948. We enjoyed these entertaining distractions but could not escape the tension held by most graduate students about what comes next. However, by 1950, I was comfortable with my graduate work and knew I would be awarded a PhD in June, the credentialing I needed to land a university-teaching job. I began looking for a position, corresponding with San Diego State University, about five hundred miles from Rhondda's parents in Santa Cruz, New York State College in Plattsburgh, the University of North Carolina, and a few others. Dr. Olson was, of course, aware of my search and brought to my attention an opening at Florida State University, a job for which he had recommended me, and I ultimately landed, beginning in the fall.

Moving on from graduate studies to real-world employment, we were in our early thirties in 1950. It was time to consider starting a family. When we left Ann Arbor in June, Rhondda was pregnant with an anticipated delivery in September.

We needed a car. New cars had been in short supply since the war as manufacturers transitioned from the war effort to making new cars. The shortage probably contributed to compliance with the "no-car" rule on campus. I added my name to a list of customers at the Ford dealership and waited. With only a week before we were scheduled to leave, my name came up, and we became the owners of a new two-door, six-cylinder car in a beautiful green at a price of about $2,200. We were on our way to Bellingham, Washington, and my nine-week summer job at Western Washington State College, now known as Western Washington University, 2,400 miles to the west. This was my first teaching job after graduating, visiting professor of child psychology, teaching mostly teachers and soon-to-be teachers.

WESTERN WASHINGTON STATE COLLEGE

Bellingham, Washington, is a coastal town at the northwest corner of the state, with Vancouver Island, Canada, to the west. The four-day trip took us through Chicago; Madison, Wisconsin; Minneapolis, Minnesota; across the northern states sharing borders with Canada; and finally into Washington. We met with little traffic, and my pregnant wife tolerated the trip well. In 1950, there were no interstates. Motels were small privately-owned establishments. As was the practice in those days, we would always examine the room before registering. Cleanliness was sometimes a problem. Generally, we paid no more than five dollars a night for a double occupancy room. We arrived in Bellingham two days before classes were to begin, found our apartment across the street from the campus, and unpacked.

The weather that summer in Bellingham was close to perfect—never too hot, never too cold—and it rarely rained. The people were hospitable. I was going to enjoy Bellingham. Norm and Marie Gronlund were old friends from Ann Arbor, and Norm had accepted a summer job there as well. On the day Norm and I were conferred our PhD's in absentia, the four of us took a drive to Mt. Baker and to a skiing facility there. Riding the ski lift to the top of the slopes that would be carpeted in snow in a few months, we descended and later stopped at a small mountain stream at the bottom of the slopes for a picnic. We toasted each other's success with slices of an enormous watermelon. Norm became a prolific writer of instructional books for an audience of teachers. The Gronlunds stayed in touch for many years.

In 1950, much of the commerce local to Bellingham was in lumber. These were "boomer" years, and new-home construction relied upon lumber. On any given day of the summer, thousands of logs in Puget Sound were taken to lumber yards or to ships. It was a sight for the summer faculty when the college treated us to a cruise to an island that was part of the Lummi Reservation. The Lummi are the original inhabitants of Washington's northernmost coast and the southern reaches of British Columbia. We were treated to salmon skewered on sticks arranged around a fire for us.

FLORIDA STATE UNIVERSITY

Summer drew to a close, and I was offered a permanent position in the psychology department, but I had a job waiting for me at Florida State University. I declined, and in August of 1950, with two weeks before I was to report to Tallahassee, we traveled south to Santa Cruz, California, to see Rhondda's parents before crossing the country.

The plan was a thousand-mile trip to visit the Millers for a few days and to then drive the 2,500 miles to my new job in Tallahassee. Route 99 carried us south, with stops in Corvallis and Eugene, Oregon, to visit friends before turning for the coast, a special experience for both of us. At times, we could see the Pacific. Finally, we came to the Golden Gate Bridge, where I described to Rhondda my passages under the bridge. It had not been that long ago, and the memories were still fresh. So much had happened in the last five years. We made our way through a much less urbanized San Francisco than today, past San Jose and Los Gatos, crossing through St. Joseph's Hill Preserve and into Santa Cruz to the home Henry and Lyn had purchased. It was not far from downtown. Again, Rhondda tolerated the trip well, but a maternity ward was clearly in her near future, forcing a decision on her making the next 2,500-mile stretch. It was Mrs. Miller who broached the possibility that the baby be born in Santa Cruz, and that I should set off without Rhondda to find an apartment and settle in, preparing our new residence for the arrival of mother and baby. Reluctant to leave her behind, it was the right and responsible decision. So I set off alone in the little Ford Mrs. Miller had filled with baby furniture, baby clothes, clothes for

Rhondda, household goods of all kinds, canned food, and even rattan furniture for the living room. Henry, being Henry, built a rack extending over the trunk on which additional furniture was stacked until the rear bumper of the car seemed perilously close to the asphalt and I insisted "no more!" On a day in late August, reminiscent of a twenties Okie in my overloaded car, I set off, driving slowly across the country, purchasing no more than five gallons of gas at each stop. I kept my speed around 50 mph, and the trip was uneventful. Rhondda was strong and in good hands, so I was not overly burdened with worry for her or the baby, though on September 25, I would wish to be in Santa Cruz.

It was a sunny day when I entered Tallahassee at daybreak, having visited my parents in Harriman on the way. I was taken with the tall pine trees and live oaks lining the road and dripping Spanish moss. Reporting to Dr. Waskom, the recently appointed chairman of the department, I was given a tour and interviewed with various deans, including Charles Davis, who later became president of Winthrop College, the next stop on my career journey. I visited the office of my immediate boss, Ralph Witherspoon. He had arranged for us to take a nice, new downstairs apartment, recently built by the recently retired psychology department chairman, Dr. Fenner. It was more than we could have hoped to have, five spacious rooms and one bath, located one block from the edge of campus. As I unloaded the car, the rear bumper rose from the hot asphalt. With a visit to Sears, I returned to the apartment with new beds, thankful for the platform Mr. Miller had constructed over the trunk, and went about arranging the furniture and setting up Ian's nursery. I called Rhondda to report on my progress. All was well on both ends of the line.

Only two years earlier, the Florida State College for Women had become Florida State University. In 1950, there were five thousand students, and Doak Campbell, for whom the FSU stadium is named, was the president. My office was in the old education and psychology building, the first building seen upon entering the front gate of campus, and it would remain my office for the next nine years. The fall semester was still a few days away, so the campus was quiet. On my second or third day, there were reports of a hurricane in the Gulf, with Tallahassee in its crosshairs. In the first year of assigning names to hurricanes in the Atlantic basin, "Baker" followed "Able" as the second such tempest of the year. We didn't get many hurricanes in Tennessee, but with the experience of Tacloban harbor only six years earlier, I prepared for it, parking the car in the shelter of a large building on campus, filling the tub with water, and strategically placing flashlights about the apartment before turning in to await the destructive forces of nature. In the morning, I awakened to a serene and sunny day. At its peak intensity, Baker's wind speed topped out at 105 mph. It veered west and made landfall at Gulf Shores Alabama, 230 miles due west. The hurricane had been predictably unpredictable by changing course and sparing Tallahassee.

My first son was born in the Catholic hospital in Santa Cruz, California, on September 25, 1950. I was in Tallahassee. Rhondda chronicled the unsympathetic care the nuns afforded her; however, Ian, born with a head full of dark hair, was healthy, and Rhondda suffered no complications. We had agreed upon a name, "Ian Douglas Smith." Without consulting me, the hospital paperwork identified my son as "Ian Douglas Miller Smith." I suppose I should not have been surprised since Rhondda also carried her mother's maiden name, "Heran." We would call him Ian, named for his soon-to-immigrate Australian uncle, to whom I had yet to be introduced. I met my son twelve days later. After a long day, in several planes, they touched down at the Tallahassee airport. I held Ian for the first time and took mother and son to our new home in Dr. Fenner's apartment.

Excepting the occasional parties in the apartment above us, Rhondda was happy with the apartment, but it was not long before we were house hunting. Lambert Heights, named for the local developer/builder Dallas Lambert, was a new subdivision not far from campus. We calculated how much house we could afford and purchased the property at 204 Edwards Street, moving from the apartment in February of 1951. FSU in 1951 was not the behemoth it is today. Getting to Edwards Street from campus, we passed a large open field on our left and a cow pasture on our right. A bridge took us over a railroad track, and Edwards Street was the second street to the right. It was a little more than half a mile drive through an area now overwhelmed by the university.

Our neighbors on Edwards Street became lifelong friends. Winthrop and Louella Kellogg, directly across the street, were famous to every psychologist in the world. They had conducted a nine-month experiment involving their son, rearing him with a chimpanzee to determine the learning limits of the chimp, comparing the animal's learning with a human.

Pictured above are Gua, the female chimpanzee, and young Donald Kellogg. They were introduced when Gua was seven months and her "brother" was ten months of age.

Ian was surrounded by other kids. Along the way, a female dalmatian puppy became a part of the family, arriving by plane from South Florida, the gift of one of my graduate students. "Lady" became Ian's constant companion.

Our Edwards Street house was constructed of concrete block with a white stucco finish and a slightly pitched roof that sometimes leaked around the chimney. It was comprised of five rooms, one bathroom, and a screened back porch. In the hallway, there was a rarely used oil-burning heater, and in the back, a carport convenient to the utility room and the clothes washer. The hot Florida sun dried clothes quickly, so a clothes dryer was superfluous as long as we had a clothesline. During my August vacation in 1956, I converted the screened porch to a "Florida room," installing white pine paneling to the walls and ceiling. A door to the backyard was installed with louvered glass windows that could be cranked open. Professionals were called in to build the fireplace. The house still stands today, although the neighborhood is a bit rundown. It is probably now a student rental.

Doug and Rhondda Smith in 1957.

We settled into routines. I taught twelve semester hours each term, and I studied continuously. Rhondda took care of her "men." Ian ate well and quickly gained weight. As an only child to this point, he enjoyed the attention and, before long, was crawling about the house. In the blink of an eye, he had evolved from baby to little boy, and Rhondda and I went from referring to him as "the baby" to referring to him as "Ian."

Before he had reached six months of age, Ian appeared to have an ear infection. His pediatrician decided to puncture his eardrum to relieve the pressure. The opening never closed, resulting in chronic ear infections throughout his childhood. I drove him to an ear specialist in Jacksonville. He scraped inside the ear, leaving Ian hurting, weary, and ready to go home. The infections followed any swimming he would do, and our trips to Jacksonville were regular. Earplugs were of no help. However, the punctured eardrum may have later earned him a 4F deferment in the draft for the war in tropical and highly humid Vietnam. Not until medical school did he solve his ear problem. A transplant for the ruptured eardrum ended the ear infections and improved his hearing.

In the mid-fifties, we decided Ian should have a brother or sister, that somehow our family was not complete, and in the spring of 1955, Rhondda happily announced she was pregnant. I had again accepted a summer session on the Western Washington faculty, this time arriving with Rhondda, a four-year-old son, and unnamed Walt in utero. Rhondda was not so far along with her pregnancy as to make the travel uncomfortable. We bought a two-wheeled trailer and loaded it with the possessions we would need during the summer. Wallace and his family were living in the countryside at the time, so we first drove to Harriman to leave Lady in their care. She would be happy there. Again, we were on a transcontinental journey. In Bellingham, we had rented the house of a faculty member who would be gone for the summer. I am not sure how much of our summer in Bellingham Ian remembers, but he may remember climbing up a Black Cherry tree in the backyard without considering how he would get down. The summer in Bellingham was again idyllic. At the end of the summer session, we retraced the route we took in August of 1950 to Santa Cruz for another visit with Rhondda's parents before again crossing the country to Harriman for a visit with my family and to retrieve Lady. It was a profitable summer. We purchased a television and a window air conditioner, both firsts for us.

The four courses I taught were generally in the areas of child and developmental psychology and in educational psychology. There were twenty-five to thirty-five students in each class. Teaching undergraduates was enjoyable, perhaps because the whole field of psychology was new to them, and they could still be excited by it. I had also committed considerable time to working with students pursuing masters or doctoral degrees, serving on eighty-five such committees while at FSU. By the time they became graduate students, they had been immersed in psychology, developed specific interests in the subject, and entered the classroom with specific goals in mind. We were also expected to do some research and to publish, which I did. The prestigious Journal of Genetic Psychology published a few of my papers. I considered writing a textbook on educational psychology and probably would have if we had remained in Tallahassee.

While we were there, I helped organize Big Bend, Inc., an investment club that also involved my neighbor John Folsom, the attorney; Homer Brinkley, an insurance guy; a medical doctor; and Jim Hunter, an employee of the state. The name derived from the bend of the Gulf coastline, twenty to thirty miles to our south. Each month, we invested $25 and met once per month for a business breakfast. I was the treasurer. We looked for property to buy and sell but made only one purchase, a city block at the old air force base that we sold the next day for a 100-percent profit. Soon after I left, Big Bend, Inc. folded.

As it is with neighborhoods, people moved out, and others moved in. The house next door had several occupants before Jake and Dorothy Endress moved in, with their son, Mike, and Dorothy's dad, a retired doctor, then around seventy-five. On the front lines, he had served as the personal doctor of General John J. "Black Jack" Pershing during World War I, while Pershing commanded the American Expeditionary Forces on the western front against Germany. Ultimately, Germany was forced to call for an armistice, which Pershing opposed, believing the war should continue until all of Germany was occupied and German militarism was permanently crushed. Occasionally, when the other family members were away, he would call me over to have a drink. His allowance was one a day, and he gleefully ignored that allowance when no one was there to monitor his intake.

When Ian had attained age three, Rhondda was driving him to school. Before arriving in Tallahassee, she had never before driven a car, and she enrolled in a driving school. Ian entered the FSU nursery school, where the children were often test subjects for faculty and students in their psychology and education projects. I was on the board that managed the school. Not without some separation anxiety, Rhondda eased him into being left there. He adjusted. Ian's test scores were always high. When he left the kindergarten program, he moved to the FSU laboratory school, where first- through fourth-grade students were taught. He was not always happy with the teachers. I suspect some were too inflexible and rigid about rules and regulations. Nevertheless, he always performed well.

Rhondda and I had an attachment to the Presbyterian church in Ann Arbor, and Rhondda sang in the choir. Before arriving in the United States, she had performed in Sydney opera houses. In Tallahassee, the three of us attended First Presbyterian Church, and again Rhondda sang in the choir, often solo. I participated in Sunday-school classes and called the pastor "Dub" Martin a friend, but we never joined the church. Sadly, Dub committed suicide, shocking the city. When the move to Rock Hill, South Carolina, was made, we joined Oakland Avenue Presbyterian Church, a block from our home at the corner of Oakland Avenue and Sumter Avenue.

When a due date was decided, Henry and Lyn came from California to be there when our second was delivered, helping me with caring for Ian and Rhondda. In the maternity ward at Tallahassee Hospital, Walter Henry Smith arrived on December 13, 1955, named for his two grandfathers. He was healthy, ate well, and grew quickly.

Walt was age three when he followed his brother into the FSU nursery school, while Ian continued at the laboratory school. Rhondda was a busy mom, delivering our children and neighbor's children to various places. Ian played Little League baseball with Sammy Morrow, who lived nearby with his father, the coach. All the neighbors and all the children knew each other. It was a good neighborhood for raising children. Neighbors visited when a new lawn mower or automobile was purchased or a new outdoor project began. I worked long hours, much of it at night at home in my study, a practice I continued for many years. My days were filled with family, reading, teaching, and sometimes travel to professional meetings, usually east of the Mississippi. For the four or five days I would be gone, Rhondda managed well without me.

Visiting Rhondda's sister Joyce Compton (seated with her children, John and Paul, standing beside her), Rhondda is on the left with Ian and Walt standing in front of her, and Doug Smith is standing on the far right.

During the Tallahassee years, 1950–1959, we made several four-and-a-half day continental crossings to visit Rhondda's parents as well as Joyce and David Compton. They had moved from Columbus, Indiana, to Santa Cruz with the intention of David helping Mr. Miller in his store. It didn't last. David took an accounting position in San Francisco, and they bought a house in the bay area south of the city.

On those trips, we stopped each evening at a small motel along fabled Route 66. The big chain hotels were still in the future, and there had been no improvement in the small establishments since our travel from Ann Arbor to Bellingham. Later trips were made in a station wagon we purchased after Walt was born. It allowed us more space. Pillows on the floorboard of the back seat were arranged so the boys could play and sleep as we traveled. They were long trips, and we learned to expect the boys to ask frequently, "Are we there yet" or "When are we going to get there?" We also visited Smith family, usually twice a year, driving north to Harriman, and sometimes they came to Tallahassee, usually in connection with a Florida vacation.

Eisenhower came to the presidency in 1953 and had signed the interstate legislation in 1956, but the first interstate highway was still many years in the future. One of the arguments for the interstate highway system was the elimination of unsafe and inefficient roads. Perhaps it was in 1953, on our Christmas visit to Harriman, we were north of Columbus, Georgia, passing an old truck loaded with long pine slabs. As we were passing, the truck driver made a left turn despite the loud protest of my car horn, collided with our Ford, and we were forced from the road. Rhondda was playing a game with Ian, who was wrapped in a small blanket on the floorboard at her feet. He suffered no injuries, but Rhondda cracked the windshield with her head, and my knees were driven into the dash, breaking off knobs and dials, perhaps figuring into my knee replacement some forty years later, perhaps not. In any event, at the time, our injuries did not appear serious. The car was towed into Columbus for repair, and I called my neighbor, Harold Cottingham, to bring us back home to celebrate Christmas in Tallahassee. Seatbelts were not standard equipment for another eleven years, and federal legislation would not make airbags mandatory until 1998.

Tallahassee was home. I enjoyed teaching, the academic atmosphere, the neighbors, and I never seriously entertained the notion of leaving. For the second time, Western Washington had made the offer of a permanent position, but I liked the job I had at FSU, and I liked the Florida weather better than the weather in Bellingham in the fall, winter, and spring seasons, when darkness comes early and wetter weather prevails.

The US Department of Health, Education, and Welfare awarded me a $250,000 grant in 1957 to start a doctoral program at FSU in School Psychology, one of about five programs to be started around the south, including Duke, Peabody, and the University of

Miami. At the time, it was one of the largest grants ever received by FSU. Spearheading the effort was the Southern Regional Education Board (SREB). For several years, I served on a planning committee, meeting monthly in Atlanta with others including Jack Boger from Virginia. Jack would later join me at Winthrop. The School Psychology program at FSU was quickly implemented.

The next year, the FSU provost determined to form several large lecture sections, combining sections of smaller classes that were being offered. The opportunity to participate was extended to me like this. If I would teach one large lecture session of educational psychology, my teaching load would be reduced from twelve to nine semester hours, from four courses to three. The numbers looked good to me, and I didn't need to think about it long before accepting. The day of my first large lecture section arrived, and among the class of about 137 students, I found the face of Mary Davis, wife of the provost, Charlie Davis. The class went well, and I discovered there were few differences between lecturing to 137 students and 35. Notably, I needed to be more precise in explanations to compensate for less class discussion to achieve clarification.

By 1959, the FSU psychology department was becoming less of a happy place. The department head, Dr. Waskom, was contending with too many ideological divisions, the likes of which have always existed in psychology and probably other disciplines. Even as I write this, the American Psychological Association (APA) seems constantly involved in healing the self-inflicted wounds that internal skirmishing produce. The national meetings of the APA reflected these divisions. The new, young PhDs brought in by the department head were little concerned with a happy department. I navigated the internal struggles well, but the skirmishes diminished the department as a place to work.

In the Tallahassee Democrat, the local paper announced the departure of Dr. Charles Davis, the university provost. It was January of 1959, and he was leaving to assume the presidency of Winthrop College in Rock Hill, South Carolina. A week after the announcement, a message was relayed by a colleague. Charlie asked me to come by his office. I was invited to join him in Rock Hill as dean of the college, to replace retiring Dean McCoy, beginning in August. I responded with "Let me think about it."

Reflecting on the offer, I recalled seeing Lincoln Memorial University Dean, Boyd Wise, then in his seventies, strolling across campus. He had retired from Centre College in Kentucky and came to LMU to be an academic dean and to teach English. Dean Wise had been my sophomore literature teacher, not a very good one, but a likable guy. It seemed like a good job to have, and my experience would recommend me for the job. I updated Dr. Davis. I wanted to visit Winthrop. I knew nothing about it, and within the week, I was on a flight from the modest Tallahassee Airport to another modest airport in Charlotte by way of Atlanta. "Willie" met me in Charlotte, a Black longtime employee of the college. He was there to take me to nearby Rock Hill and the college in a twenty-year-old Ford. The college's "fleet" was small and old. I asked Willie if many of the faculty had been there long. Faculty retention is a legitimate question for a new dean. He replied, "Yes, sir, some of them too long!" I was delivered to the president's mansion at a corner of the campus on Oakland Avenue.

The house was occupied by Dr. Henry Sims and his wife, Trish. He had come to the president's office in the late 1940s from the South Carolina Senate, where he served as chairman of the senate education committee. The board had turned to Chairman Sims when a vacancy occurred, though he had no special preparation for the job as a lawyer from Orangeburg, South Carolina. The Sims' were very kind to me, inviting me to their home for dinner. Sitting at the dining-room table, eating and chatting, I looked beyond Henry, seeing a large settlement crack in the wall. The house and the college needed work.

Winthrop had its origins in Columbia in 1886, when a talented school superintendent, David Bancroft Johnson, recognized a need for teachers to be better trained and petitioned Boston Philanthropist, Robert C. Winthrop, chairman of the Peabody Fund, for seed money to form a school with a mission to train White women as teachers. Known then as Winthrop Training School, it opened with an entering class of twenty-one women. State support for the school and its move to Rock Hill came in 1895. When I arrived in 1959, it remained a college for women, and that did not change until 1974.

For some years, the college had been on a "censured list" maintained by the American Association of University Professors (AAUP) owing to a lingering rift between the college administration and the college faculty. Dr. Sims was not disturbed by this significant problem and, in fact, viewed the AAUP with some opprobrium—a view that devalued the faculty as a part of the college community. I toured the campus and also visited Dean McCoy at the dean's house. It was abundantly clear that whoever filled the positions of dean and president had a great deal of work to do, beginning with securing more money for campus maintenance and repairing damaged relations with faculty and staff. I had the opportunity to build something important and necessary, teaching teachers and improving the education of students exponentially. A move to Rock Hill held promise. I could accomplish something significant. From the perspective of a teacher in an undergraduate setting, I saw greater room for self-expression and seeing immediate results from teaching.

On the return trip to Tallahassee, my thoughts were dominated by the offer. I talked it over with Rhondda. We reviewed what we would be leaving, proximity to the beach and south Florida and enduring friendships. I had been a full professor for over a year in a school that, one day, might achieve a degree of prestige. The boys had easy access to a good laboratory school. It was all weighed against the potential for us in Rock Hill. Characteristic of Rhondda throughout her life, she was always ready for a change, always ready to go. The suggestion of a trip was always met with "Sure, I'll be ready when you are," and her luggage would appear by the door. I accepted the job.

WINTHROP COLLEGE

I continued at Florida State through the spring semester and began my Winthrop job on August 1, 1959, a month ahead of Charlie Davis assuming the president's office. We set our moving date, Thursday, July 30, 1959. As the date approached, we packed our belongings, made arrangements with a moving company, closed bank accounts, and forwarded our mail to the dean's house at Winthrop. A Live Oak stood near the entrance to the driveway of our house on Edwards Street, and an overhanging limb had to be cut before the moving van could get near the door. I placed my ladder underneath the tree, climbed to the proper height, and began sawing. Perhaps misjudging the physics involved, the limb took an unfortunate twist as it fell the short distance to the ground, knocking me and my stepladder to the ground. The stepladder was unaffected. I, on the other hand, had suffered a broken left wrist, requiring a cast, and a painful cut on my upper lip, requiring stitches. Ian had witnessed the whole thing. Packing was a little slower, but we drove into our new hometown with a well-loaded trailer.

The Smith family entered Rock Hill the day after we departed Tallahassee and proceeded to unload the trailer. I worked with one hand. We were followed closely by our movers, who pulled up to the house early on the morning of August 1, and they quickly filled the house with our furniture. Neighbors came by to help with keeping the boys occupied while we worked. We were young and strong and fearless, and we looked forward to a new job, a new town, and new friends; and if you don't count the broken wrist and driving with one hand for 450 miles, it was an easy move.

The dean's house was two stories, with wood siding and a broad front porch in the Southern tradition, at the corner of Park Avenue and Cherry Road, near the Home Economics building. The rent was $100 per month, and it included water, heat, and electricity. The heat was generated from the college's centrally located power plant, delivering steam to the pipes under the house and the old-fashioned radiators located at strategic places in the house. We would wake up on winter mornings to the knocking and rattling of the pipes as they expanded. The house had no air-conditioning; however, a large overhead fan in the ceiling of the hallway could cool the entire house, pulling air through open windows. Even in the dog days of summer, we slept in relative comfort. The second day there, I found the fig tree near the free-standing garage in the backyard. Eating the fresh figs I pulled directly from that tree, I was punished by a night of stomach cramps and was visited by a doctor the next day on a house call. His diagnosis, too many figs!

Dr. Hampton Jarrell, chairman of the English department, and Mrs. Jarrell, lived across the street, with a professor of music next door to them. A year later, Lady and another dog would kill the Jarrell's cat. Rhondda painted a still life of roses for them and asked for forgiveness. The cat was part of the Jarrell family, and they were upset by the loss but allowed themselves to forgive us, and maybe Lady too.

Next door to us were Bill and Mary Long. With his wife's assistance, Bill was the longtime chairman of the theater program. In the 1990s, Mary hosted a popular public television program on historical places in South Carolina. They had met at *The Lost Colony*, an outdoor drama at the Manteo, North Carolina, Waterside Theater. They had three children, all older than our boys. With the benefit of having watched his parents at work, William Ivey Long, Jr. became well known as a Tony Award-winning costume designer associated with more than seventy Broadway productions, television shows, operas, and films.

Walking to the end of Park Street in front of our house, Walt turned right and went to the second building on his right each morning to the nursery school operated by the college. Ian's walk to Winthrop Training School (WTS) took him left from Park and across Oakland Avenue, about three blocks. He was in fourth grade. WTS spanned from kindergarten through grade twelve and was recognized as a prodigious college preparatory school. The citizens of Rock Hill were proud of it. In later years, Ian would look back upon it and declare that some of the best teachers in his life were there, but it was short-lived. State funds dried up in 1966. It became hard to demonstrate that the school was the best use of state money, and the school was cut back to sixth grade. Ian entered Rock Hill High School the next year.

A few short years after moving into the house on Park, it was pulled down for the construction of Lee Wicker Hall on its site. We had moved to 638 Oakland Avenue, across from my office in Tillman Hall, named for Benjamin Ryan Tillman. Also known as "Pitchfork Ben," he had been the state's governor, a US senator, and an unapologetic racist firebrand, defending lynching on the floor of the United States Senate. He led the paramilitary "Red Shirts" in South Carolina, which today would be labeled a terrorist group, most notably in the Hamburg Massacre of 1876. In 1873, well into Reconstruction, the Red Shirt movement in the defeated confederate South was born out of the acknowledgment that it was not possible to outvote formerly disenfranchised African Americans and a belief that White men should be restored to their antebellum preeminent political power. Known as "rifle clubs," Tillman's "Sweetwater Sabre Club" is known to have intimidated, assaulted, and killed would-be Black voters and political figures. Tillman died four months before I was born in 1918.

What do I do now? I wondered as I sat at the dean's desk for the first time. Fay Hoke and her part-time assistant, Hester Broughton, were there to answer that question, and within a week, I had settled into the job. My office was old, large, and comfortable. Fay and Hester were friendly to the faculty and staff, knowledgeable, and efficient. There was no end to the parade of issues to be addressed, and the first day set the table for what was to follow. The head of the Department of Mathematics resigned to take a job at a Midwestern school. On the heels of that vacancy, another developed in the position of chairman of the Department of Education. Two vital positions had to be filled with a month to go before the fall semester. Winthrop was facing a problem that was becoming an academic epidemic. The fix for these two positions were Band-Aids, hastily applied, but nonetheless a fix, and one that allowed us time to consider better answers.

Graduate schools in 1959 were producing doctorates in all disciplines, but many new PhDs were electing to remain at their schools for post-doctoral fellowships, generally working on research projects for their faculty advisors. At the same time, baby boom students were pouring into colleges and universities, and professors were needed to teach them. Graduate-school professors were not sympathetic to the needs of the undergraduate institutions. They aggressively held on to their new PhDs. As a consequence, deans at undergraduate schools, like Winthrop, were challenged to attract the new PhDs to their campuses. I was at Winthrop for nine years (1959–1968). Faculty recruitment was to be the most difficult component of my job. Mathematics, physics, and economics were especially difficult to fill at a women's undergraduate college, complicated by the prevailing perception that women were neither suited for nor interested in those fields. Indeed, the culture had done little to encourage high-school girls in those studies.

Faculty recruitment was a constant challenge throughout the 1960s, taking me to most of the larger southern universities, a few in the northern border states, and in the Midwest to find and interview prospects for Winthrop. I succeeded, but at a cost of personal wear and tear and absence from my young family. A week's recruiting tour might yield one or two new faculty members, but the student body at Winthrop had a trajectory of steady growth. The need for new faculty never ceased, and the pressure to find them was unrelenting. Enrollment at Winthrop grew from about 1,100 in 1959 to nearly 3,000 by 1968. Without question, my nine years as the academic dean at Winthrop were my hardest working years.

It was a time when Rock Hill and Charlotte were separated by some countryside. Rock Hill was a small southern town, people were friendly, children could play safely and ride their bikes anywhere. Being associated with the college provided ready-made friends for Rhondda and me as well as for the boys. Rhondda played bridge with faculty wives and became particularly close to Pix Drennan, an Australian, with whom she shared a great deal in common. Pix was the wife of Jud Drennan, the college business manager. They also met during the war when Jud was stationed there.

At the college farm, as it was known, there was fishing at Winthrop Lake, gatherings at the "Shack," which was more substantial than the name would imply, and golf at a nine-hole course adjacent to the farm, given to the college by a local firm. The farm was a little more than half a mile from the house, at the other end of Sumter Avenue. Rhondda and the boys would play golf there, and a few times I took the boys there to fish. In warm weather, Walt and his best friend, Scott, whose father Bob Bristow was an English professor and scratch golfer, were fixtures at the golf course. Occasionally, at the shack Rhondda and I were chaperones at Winthrop dances, and we stood in long reception lines to welcome new students to the school.

I joined the Kiwanis Club, and we ate at the Elks Club on some Sundays. We became members of Oakland Avenue Presbyterian Church. I would sit in the pews with the boys, and we watched and listened to Rhondda sing in the choir. Walt became a Cub Scout, meeting his friend, David Klein, son of the pastor. Rhondda was also invited to sing solos on special occasions at the Episcopal Church downtown.

In short order, the majority of faculty members at Winthrop were my hires. Jack Boger was convinced in my second year to leave Virginia to take the position as chairman of the Department of Education, which, true to the school's original mission, was one of the largest departments. We had met and worked together on the Southern Regional Education Board committee on School Psychology when I was at FSU. He was a prized hire for me and a good friend for many years. I enjoyed many friendships with faculty members, particularly in the psychology department. I am thinking of Harley Scott, Ron Laffitte, and Bill Murdy, and knowing them provided for a rich social life. Charlie Huff became head of the Mathematics department when he walked into my office and declared he wanted to leave Auburn University to return to South Carolina. He was anxious to enroll his mentally challenged daughter in a special school in the state. Like most "families," there were quarrels. At the monthly meeting of department heads in my office, they badgered relentlessly, but when we adjourned, we were all friends. College administration in an undergraduate school was far more fulfilling than my job as a professor of psychology at FSU.

During all my years at Winthrop, President Charlie Davis was careful to include me in all his meetings with business officers each month and took me with him to meet with legislators and other officials in Columbia. In fact, the business data were sent to me, and I prepared most of the institutional reports. I served on committees of the dean of Women's Affairs, including the disciplinary committee that meted out sentences for infractions of college rules, like drinking, dress-code violations, delinquent check-in at night— all issues that had long ago been abandoned at other universities and colleges and would only survive at Winthrop for a few more months. The dean of women retired and was replaced by Iva Gibson from Montevallo, Alabama, who relaxed the rules. I knew and understood every aspect of the college's operations.

MEXICO

The summer of 1961 arrived, and our country's long involvement in Vietnam began with the government sending nine hundred military advisors to Saigon. My family was on the way to Monterey, Mexico, where I served on the summer board of visitors at the prestigious Instituto Tecnologico for a week. It was warm, and the boys were in the swimming pool daily. Our lodgings were in an apartment on campus, and we ate Mexican cuisine in the college dining hall. A Mexican faculty member and his family took us to a park atop a nearby mountain for a picnic. Only six at the time, Walt remembers him as "Felix," the name of a popular black-and-white cat cartoon character on television. Of course, everything on television was black and white in our house at the time. The children could only speak their respective languages but seemed able to communicate and played together all afternoon. When the week was over, we drove on to Mexico City, about 300 km south, allowing us to take in the Mexican countryside. George and Eloise Crow hitched a ride with us as far as a small nearby town, where they wanted to do some shopping. I later offered Dr. Crow the position of head of the Foreign Languages department at Winthrop, and he accepted.

SOUTHEAST ASIA

In the summer of 1963, I spent three weeks touring Southeast Asia with a stipend from the US Department of Education. While in Cuba eighteen years earlier, I had expected to visit Japan, courtesy of the US Navy. Beginning my tour there, I am not sure what I expected to find in the small-island country that made war with the world. A distinct culture with a language that shares no similarity with English, my preparation began with learning a few necessary words of the intimidating language. The country is dotted with temples and pagodas, the towers with multiple tiers and upward curling eaves, frequently located near Buddhist monasteries. I toured many historic and culturally significant places and took a boat ride through Japan's inland sea, an 8,959-square-mile body of water separating three of Japan's five main islands. I was there to do a job. I visited two universities and talked with a number of professors before flying to Seoul, Korea, on KAL for a week of touring universities there. Then I was off to Taiwan. I had been invited to speak at a dinner with the Department of Psychology at the National University. In Hong Kong, I dined with a college president and did some sightseeing with my guide and host, a former Winthrop college student and Hong Kong native. I spent a night in Tokyo before boarding a flight to Anchorage, Alaska, for a visit to a nearby glacier. It was June and it was daylight for twenty-four hours a day. Finally, my three-week adventure was over, and I was on my way home to my family.

EUROPE

The year 1965 was another turbulent one. The Vietnam War was escalating, race riots erupted in the Watts section of Los Angeles, US forces occupied the Dominican Republic, and Malcom X (f/Little) was assassinated. It was also the year that the arch in St. Louis was completed, the space race was in full swing, and Muhammad Ali defeated Sonny Liston in the ring. With that stormy backdrop, our family sailed out of New York harbor aboard the SS *Constitution* on a course to Casablanca, where in the previous March, the Moroccan Army, under newly installed King Hassan II, fired on student protesters. They were demanding the right to public higher education for Moroccans, opposing the proclamation of the country's Minister of Education that would prevent 60 percent of students from continuing their education after age seventeen. Our stop there was brief. We would proceed past Gibraltar and disembark in Naples, in the south of Italy. Launched in September 1950, the Constitution was retired in 1995. It now rests on the ocean floor seven hundred nautical miles north of the Hawaiian Islands after sinking on my birthday in 1997 while under tow to be scrapped.

We toured Naples and its surroundings, then traveled by bus to Rome and its countless tourist destinations. We found the ancient ruins, and Ian and Walt replayed Brutus murdering Julius Caesar in the place it is said to have happened. There is a tribute to Romulus and Remus, the twin brothers in Roman mythology who founded Rome, a wolf suckling two boys atop a large column. Ian would be reminded of this later when asked about the brothers on *Classroom*

Quiz, a televised contest between three-member high-school teams. Representing Rock Hill High School, he was asked about the twins. Looking at the camera, he was a black-and-white deer in headlights.

Renting a car, I drove the family to Florence, Milan, Geneva through Germany, and to Amsterdam, finally arriving at The Hague. From there, a ferry took us to Harwich, England, and we rented another car. We traveled to central England and Nottingham, where we found Sherwood Forest of Robin Hood fame, before driving on to Edinburgh. We crossed back through England to the small town in Wales for which Rhondda was named, pausing for a picture of her posing by a sign bearing her name and that of the small town on the banks of the Rhondda River. A little more than a year after Rhondaa posed by that sign, about three miles away, 109 children and five of their teachers would lie dead under 140,000 cubic yards of coal mining waste slurry. In the nearby village of Aberfan, a pile of coal waste ("tip") had been building on a mountain slope over a natural spring for eight years. Just as lessons were beginning at Pantglas Junior School on October 21, 1966 it towered 111 feet over the village. An extended period of rain added more water until the integrity of the tip was no longer sustainable and a slide engulfed the school and a row of houses.

London was next on our itinerary. If it is a tourist sight in London, we probably stood in front of it for a picture. We stayed a few days before climbing aboard a TWA flight to New York, there to cap off the trip with a visit to the New York World's Fair before driving back to Rock Hill. We had been away from home for six weeks. Ian was fourteen, and Walt was nine. Both have had good memories of the trip, and taking the boys to see some of the world might have been our greatest parental accomplishment.

ROCK HILL

I was a smoker; cigars regularly after being spoiled in Cuba and the occasional cigarette. That changed. I found myself reaching for a cigarette when I sat down to talk to faculty or guests. Then, in the mid-sixties, the US Surgeon General issued his report linking tobacco use to cancer, and by the following year, cigarette packages distributed in the country began to carry the now-familiar health warning. It came at a time when I was off cigarettes due to a cold and sore throat that I reasoned would not be helped by smoking. I heeded the warning, never again to light up, though my conviction to quit was challenged by increasing stress on the job.

My stress was directly attributable to Charlie Davis, who I credit with giving me the opportunity to be a better college administrator. At the same time, Charlie worked fewer hours because of it. Winthrop grew steadily, and the faculty grew stronger, and though he was the boss, the faculty looked to me to get things done. Consequently, his role as president was diminished. This was not helped by talk that the president of the women's college was a "womanizer." In 1966, board members John Martin and John T. Roddy, as a committee to investigate the matter, called and questioned me. In Small Town, South Carolina, in the sixties, people were inquisitive about the personal lives of local leaders, and the president of a women's college was likely under greater scrutiny than others. With no hesitation, I responded that I had no knowledge of Charlie's misbehaving with the woman in question.

As we entered the late 1960s, Charlie and I were on a collision course, and increasingly, I felt it was time for me to go. His judgment was not always sound. His evaluation of people seemed colored by irrelevant factors. I also sensed he was beginning to be uncomfortable with me. My stock with the faculty, staff, and community was high, perhaps too high for his subordinate. It was in this climate that I received inquiries about my availability for the presidency of two schools, Salisbury State College on the flat eastern shore of Maryland and Western Carolina University in Cullowhee, located in the mountains of North Carolina. I quietly went about the business of making my dossier available to both. Ian was near the end of his high-school years, and Walt was a rising seventh grader, so a change of schools was in the cards for him either way. The time for a move was right.

Both institutions were visited, and I spoke with their respective board members. Cullowhee is on the Tuckasegee River, and the surroundings are scenic, especially in autumn, but the town had little to offer outside of the campus of Western Carolina. Salisbury was a small town as well but convenient to Annapolis, Washington D.C., and Baltimore, and the beaches at Ocean City. The Wicomico River ran through Salisbury to the Chesapeake. Walter Cronkite, who presided over CBS evening news in the sixties and seventies, was said to have his sailboat docked on the Wicomico. I had every indication that an offer was forthcoming from Western Carolina, but Rhondda had made clear that she had no interest in living in an isolated mountain town, though it would have put us within 160 miles of family in Harriman. Having lived her life primarily in more populous cities, Rhondda was a "city girl," and I understood that the idea of living in a small mountain town held no appeal for her. The offer from Salisbury arrived, and I accepted.

SALISBURY STATE COLLEGE

Like Winthrop, Salisbury State College was a small school with fewer than eight hundred students that emphasized teacher training. It held promise. The location, twenty-five to thirty miles from Ocean City, Maryland, would attract students, locally and from the urban centers on the western side of the Chesapeake. Properly managed, it could become a coveted institution in the state. I was offered a salary of $18,000 per year, a house, car, and entertainment expense reimbursement. Perched on a lonely hill on the otherwise flat landscape of the area, the president's house was two stories and all brick in a federalist style on a very large lot at 1301 Camden Avenue. It was a short walk to my office. There were nine rooms and three bathrooms, with a full basement, where I could exercise in winter. We were comfortable there. The car was another matter, a black 1967 Plymouth with no air-conditioning. Summers on the Eastern Shore can be punishing. Nearly equidistant between the Chesapeake and the Atlantic, it was also humid. When I drove to Baltimore up Route 50 and over the Chesapeake Bay Bridge through Annapolis, I was frequently accompanied by a local board member. She was an elderly lady whose makeup seemed to dissolve in the summer heat.

Ian was graduating from high school at a time when St. Thomas University in Houston was scheduled for reaccreditation, and I needed to go to Houston to make arrangements for the committee. The school is only a few blocks from Rice, so Ian accompanied me on the trip. He had applied to Rice, and this was his campus visit. He had previously toured Clemson and Princeton. I went to do my preparations at St. Thomas and later met Ian for lunch in the Rice dining hall. "This campus is spooky," he said, probably owing to the paucity of students during the summer session. After lunch, he conspired with some summer-term students in one of the dorms, dropping water balloons from the room on the unsuspecting student pedestrians below. In the late afternoon, I returned and was greeted by "I want to go to Rice," and he did at the age of sixteen, declaring his major in physics.

Walt accepted the move to Salisbury with little reluctance. He made friends, Mark Cook as primary among them. Mark lived within bicycling distance down Camden Avenue. His father was the director of a business development group, The Greater Salisbury Committee, and a good person for me to know. Walt attended James M. Bennett Junior High School, riding a school bus that stopped at our driveway and was chronically late in delivering children to school. He joined a scout troop that met at the Episcopal Church downtown, and he got involved in the youth program at the Presbyterian church. The youth minister was Roger Gullick, who later stood at the pulpit at First Presbyterian Church of Florence.

In Maryland, the four-year state colleges were managed by the state college board of trustees, though the University of Maryland was managed by a separate board. To say the board was "stingy" would be generous. It suffered from the strong central control of Baltimore and Annapolis and a stifling, heavy bureaucracy. There were rigid rules for everything concerning money, personnel, promotions, and building construction—sometimes with unfathomable results. Little local discretion was allowed. Salisbury State, remotely located on the Eastern Shore, was a low priority. At the same time, our seclusion did allow us some freedom to operate outside of the constant scrutiny of the Annapolis-Baltimore bureaucracy. The soon-to-be-disgraced governor, Spiro Agnew, had little interest in the state colleges and never visited the campus. Before occupying that office, he was a Baltimore County executive; in that position, creating a kickback scheme he took with him to the governor's mansion and then to Washington when he became the thirty-ninth vice president on the Republican Nixon/Agnew ticket. When he was investigated by the US Attorney for Maryland, Agnew resigned and pled nolo contendere ("no contest") to charges of tax evasion, meaning he was not admitting guilt but would not contest the charges. During my two years in Maryland, we built one women's dormitory. The construction took years of lobbying, planning, and finally construction. Funding was a long-term problem, but other problems had to be addressed quickly.

The dean of Salisbury State had resigned just prior to my arrival on campus. This was only two months ahead of the fall semester. Again, I applied a Band-Aid, asking the chemistry department chairman to serve as acting dean for a year. He only held a master's degree, but he was friendly and would be accepted by the faculty for a year. My predecessor as president was Dr. Wilbur Devilbiss, who came from the School of Education at the University of Maryland in College Park. It appeared that he had made a practice of hiring faculty from the local high schools. There were few doctorates among the faculty. The number of students was trending upwards. We needed more professors and better-qualified professors to strengthen the school. The college was in need of an overhaul on multiple levels.

I set about converting the curriculum of the former teacher's college to that of a liberal arts institution. All these efforts should have been carried out by the previous administration, and I concluded that Dr. Devilbiss did not want the school to grow. In the short two years I was there, I was successful in changing the direction of the school, with the help of a friend and colleague I lured from Winthrop. Jack Baker was the assistant to the academic dean in Rock Hill, and in June of 1969, he moved with his family to Salisbury. His experience at Winthrop had prepared him well, and he made a strong impression as academic dean at Salisbury. Delores Miller was my irreplaceable assistant, who had worked at the college for seventeen years and knew the college and the town well. Jack and Delores were later invited to follow me to Florence.

Driving the country roads of the Eastern Shore on Saturdays, we passed by wading birds in the marshlands and rode the Upper and Whitehaven ferries operated for free by Wicomico County, appreciating the wild birds and beauty of the land. I liked the area and wondered why its population had not swelled with people similarly affected by its charm. The answer might be found by looking at the map. The people on the Eastern Shore might once have been described as "provincial" before the bridges from Norfolk and Annapolis were built. The 17.6-mile Chesapeake Bay Bridge-Tunnel, after four years of construction, opened for business in 1964, only four years before our arrival. Four man-made islands, each the size of a football field, connected the bridge sections of Route 13 with tunnels at depths ranging from twenty-five to one hundred feet. Known locally as the "Bay Bridge," Route 50 didn't connect the urban western shore with the rural eastern shore until 1952. Maryland had not discovered its Eastern Shore, and an Eastern-Shore culture developed. In fact, there have been several attempts to secede from Maryland to become the state of Delmarva, for the three states having a piece of the peninsula, the most recent attempt being in 1998.

Shifting the curriculum focus from teaching college to liberal arts was spearheaded by Jack Baker. "Marketing" the location as being in Maryland's beach vacation area, rather than the farm belt, was rewarded with broadening student recruitment. Enrollment numbers climbed immediately. The school was moving in an encouraging direction.

The Maryland experience was sometimes frustrating, but it did pay dividends for my future. In those two years, the state was involved in developing a ten-year plan for all higher education institutions in Maryland, all of which were fully partnered in the planning. A professional firm went to each campus and worked closely with its people in crafting the plan. I was deeply engaged in the plan and learned a great deal. I had previous experience serving on committees of the Southern Association of Colleges and Schools (SACS) on campuses across the South. The Maryland-planning experience provided new ideas for matching facilities with student needs, adding to my resume for the job in Florence at a new school with the working name "Marion State College."

Dr. James Morris was the director of the South Carolina Commission on Higher Education in 1969. We had been friends since my days at Winthrop. He called me in August. The new college was in the works, and he asked if I would think about returning to the Palmetto State. The fall semester at Salisbury was not far off. The new college was slated to open in June, 1970, but planning would need to be underway long before. I was acquainted with then-governor, Bob McNair, who had recommended me to Maryland State Senator, Mary Nock, of Salisbury for the position there. Jim and Bob had me at the top of their list to plan a new college. Only thirteen months into the Salisbury job before the call came, at age fifty-one, I expected to retire on the Eastern Shore. While the bureaucracy of the Maryland system was a disincentive to stay, unnecessarily cramping what could be accomplished, my experience at Winthrop informed me that the South Carolina system was closer to the other end of the bureaucratic spectrum. I thought of Winthrop's first president, David Bancroft Johnson. Interestingly, he was born in the dormitory at LaGrange Female College, where his father was the founding president. Johnson went on to found Winthrop, his own women's college. I imagined the experience it must have been to build a college unfettered, without the delay of convincing others whose credentials did not include knowledge or experience in building a college. If the responsibility of starting the new college was principally mine, I could design it as my previous decades in higher education had taught me. There would be no faculty to dictate curriculum decisions, no business office controlling business decisions, and no students to consult about rules and regulations.

Ian was off at Rice and really did not figure in my calculations. On the other hand, Walt had been pulled from Rock Hill only two years earlier and would confront another change. Rhondda had seen my frustrations with the Maryland bureaucracy firsthand, and as expected, she was characteristically ready to go. The job was mine if I wanted it. After a few trips to Columbia and Florence, I decided that when the offer was officially made, I would accept. The Maryland board would not be happy with my departure after only two years, but I answered that reservation with a question. How many educators are given the opportunity to be the founding president of a college? But there was another important consideration that sealed my decision to go. When I left Winthrop, I left eighteen years in the South Carolina Retirement System. It did not figure in my decision to go to Salisbury. Maryland did not allow interstate transfer of retirement credits. When I reached sixty-five and had added my fourteen years in Florence to the South Carolina retirement credits, the account became very important to me.

Although Jim Morris and Governor McNair had made it clear I was offered the job, it was a necessary part of the hiring process that I meet with the soon-to-be board of trustees for the new college in October of 1969, though the board would not actually take office until the new college would be legally founded on July 1, 1970. James Rogers, publisher of the *Florence Morning News*, was the newly elected chairman of the board. He made the formal offer, and I accepted. My responsibilities swelled, and my life suddenly lurched forward to meet the challenges of running two colleges.

Most free weekends were spent flying from Washington National on Eastern Airlines or driving south on Route 13, across the Chesapeake Bay Bridge-Tunnel, through Emporia, Virginia, on US 58, and Interstate 95 to Florence. It became a very familiar road, and I had my favorite stops, including an ice-cream parlor in Emporia. Starting a college requires enormous planning, for buildings, curriculum, libraries, laboratories, faculty, staff, student rules and regulations, and budgets. The list really goes on as the evolution of a college unfolds. I was grateful to have Jack Baker to share in the planning and travel to Florence.

The legislation creating the new college stipulated that the college would begin with only freshmen, sophomores, and juniors, and the senior class would be added in the second year of operation. I opted to write the catalog defining the curriculum and the student manual. Jack wrote the faculty manual. We both brought to the table long experience in college administration and the preparation of these and many other foundational documents, though never before without the contributions of faculty, staff, or student committees. "Decision by committee" is an expression seldom used favorably. We did not have time for decisions by committee. These foundational documents were needed months in advance of student enrollment and faculty hiring, affording students and faculty time to make informed decisions about coming to the school. After hours, weekends, and holidays were dedicated to this work.

Although our otherwise leisure time was spent planning for the new college, Jack and I were busy with the everyday work of running Salisbury State. It appeared to be thriving. Applications for admission steadily increased. My work on the Maryland State College's master plan for higher education continued with frequent meetings of the college presidents in the Annapolis office, and I was often involved with appearances before legislative committees that addressed higher-education issues. I became familiar with the Maryland legislators, including Paul Sarbanes, who later went to the US Senate. He grew up in Salisbury. There was also Rogers Morton, a rising national figure from the Eastern Shore at Easton, who served as US Secretary of the Interior and as US Secretary of Commerce.

Adding to the sense of a college community, Rhondda and I maintained a regular schedule of inviting one or more academic departments to the president's house for dinner each Friday night. The practice allowed us to stay informed about the lives of faculty and staff members. The events also included townspeople. The college Food Service Director appeared to enjoy the chance to offer his services in a more formal environment than the college cafeteria afforded. The success of these weekly events might have been measured by our fluency with the first names of most faculty members. Informality was appreciated as it had been at Winthrop.

Ian flew in for the extended holidays, touching down at the Baltimore Friendship Airport. We had purchased for him a 1969 Ford Mustang, and during the Christmas break of that year, he pulled up the long drive of the president's house at 1301 Camden Avenue, arriving during one of those faculty dinners. My son had fully embraced the protest culture of the late 1960s. He was wearing a fringed leather jacket in the style of Dennis Hopper in *Easy Rider* (1969), blue jeans, leather moccasins for shoes, and a headband held his long hair in place. I welcomed him to the room filled with well-attired adult faculty with "how chief," my palm raised in the peace gesture of so many westerns. He later let me know the greeting and the gesture made him aware that the outfit was ridiculous and that he was aping the student culture of the time. Salisbury was a long way from Haight Ashbury. Student protests were hardly noticeable on the Eastern Shore, though one government official, who was invited to speak on campus, had his car rocked by students. It lasted only a few minutes. The speaker chuckled about it, and the campus police were livid.

Ian graduated from Rice in 1970, and his family was there for commencement. It was our last opportunity to visit him in Houston. There were some signs of student rebellion. The Rice students sometimes demonstrated their opposition to the Vietnam War in the form of inappropriate commencement attire...barefoot, without shirts and ties, but wearing the cap and gown. Ian was made aware that after making the 1,500-mile drive to see him cross the graduation stage, we would be disappointed if he failed to give the moment the sober dignity it deserved. If there were any signs of protest, they were hidden by the commencement gown. We were proud.

Graduation from Rice was followed by a fellowship in oceanography at the Massachusetts Institute of Technology (MIT) and the Woods Hole Institute on the Cape. He moved into a tiny apartment, little more than a room, a closet, and a bathroom, but it was near the MIT campus. His course work at MIT went well, but his heart was not in it, and he opted not to pursue oceanography, despite the pleas of his professors. I may have pushed oceanography on him. Ian came back to Florence to rethink his future.

By February of 1970, the location for the new school was decided. We had settled on the former campus of the University of South Carolina at Florence, allowing us to use the existing Stokes Hall and Wallace Hall and the surrounding acreage for the construction that was to begin. Formerly the Gregg family cotton plantation, the Wallace family had donated the land for USC Florence. It came with two surviving slave cabins built before 1831 and occupied by as many as fourteen people until the 1950s. They are listed on the National Register of Historic places (1974), and one was to be donated to the Smithsonian before being damaged by Hurricane Hugo (1989).

The site selection came with an anecdote. On March 11, 1958 (twelve years earlier), Captains Kulka and Koehler were flying a US Air Force B-47 with an atomic bomb suspended over the bomb bay doors. A fault light in the cockpit indicated a bomb harness-locking pin was not engaged, and Kulka investigated. As he reached around the bomb to pull himself up, he mistakenly pulled on the emergency release pin. The bomb dropped to the bomb bay doors, its weight forced them open, and it dropped 15,000 feet onto the Gregg family farm, about 2,500 feet from Stokes Hall at the regional USC campus. Fortunately, the fissile nuclear core was carried separately, but the conventional high explosives detonated, destroying a playhouse and severely damaging the Gregg's home. It left a crater about 70 feet across and 35 feet deep. The Gregg girls were about two hundred yards away, playing with their cousin, Ella Davies, who was left with a scar on her face. Ian went out with Ella in the seventies. The story conjures images of Slim Pickens in *Doctor Strangelove*.

Delores Miller, my assistant at Salisbury, agreed to go to the new college as assistant to the president, and she became the first person at the college to begin full-time employment in November 1969, when she resigned at Salisbury and came to the new school and served as the official representative of the new administration. She assumed occupancy of a small office in Stokes Hall. Because the college would not officially exist until July 1 of the following year, she was paid by the Commission on Higher Education, the agency assigned to apply the $200,000 appropriated by the legislature for the planning and preparation costs for the new school.

The planning team, composed of board members, architects, and others, was assembled. They included Jim Rogers (chairman), Dick Wilkins (Florence architect), Richard Moses (board member), Delores Miller (assistant to the president), and a well-known campus planner, Richard K. Webel, an architect with Innocenti & Webel, having its offices on Long Island in New York. He flew from Florence to Salisbury to work with me on our dining-room table in the house on the hill. Webel, Wilkins, and I put our respective visions for the campus together in imaginative drawings and elevations. This was the beginning of the master plan. When the two-day work session ended, the emerging plan governed every step of campus development for over a decade. I drove the group to the small Salisbury airport. They boarded their single-engine plane and were wheels up into typical February Eastern Shore weather, cool rain, and low visibility.

Budget fights are part of the job, and the first fight was just around the corner. It was May of 1970, and I was still at Salisbury when I got a call from board chairman, Jim Rogers. The legislature was working to complete its budget, but it had only authorized $985,000 of the $1,500,000 that the college had planned on and Governor McNair had proposed. Jim asked that I come down together to meet with the governor. The additional money had to be found. I was in the midst of winding down my relationship with Salisbury, and I did not have time to drive to Florence. He asked if I could take one-day off for the trip, and I agreed. He called me back. Jim convinced the governor to send the state plane to the Eastern Shore to bring me to Columbia. These were the "get-it-done" people on our team. I met the plane at the Salisbury airport the next morning. The only passenger on the plane, in both directions, I met with Jim Rogers, Governor McNair, the director of the Commission on Higher Education, and the state auditor, Pat Smith. When I was given the floor, I provided a detailed one-year budget for the new college. Line by line, there was no fat. We needed the full $1,500,000. The governor agreed. He turned to Pat Smith and said, "Well, Pat, it looks like we've got to find some more money." Jim Morris and Pat Smith offered an answer. The new college would retain all its fees and tuition income as opposed to turning it all over to the state treasurer as was the practice to defray the state's costs of bond indebtedness that funded college-construction projects. Those funds would be applied instead to the regular budget of the college. We had an agreement. I was home in time for dinner. Fees and tuitions were retained in this manner for my thirteen years at the school. Ultimately, our first-year budget was about $1,350,000.

At long last, my presidential responsibilities at Salisbury State were coming to a close, and we prepared for the move to Florence and new responsibilities. The Maryland board had named a new president, Norman Crawford. I met with him and passed along all the information I could impart. We were leaving the college, now known as Salisbury University. Because I had accumulated unused vacation time, we were able to leave the Eastern Shore a few days ahead of my July 1 employment date. With warm feelings for the place but little regret, we headed south on Route 13.

FRANCIS MARION COLLEGE

Jim Rogers and I went house hunting in early spring of 1970. A proper president's house would need to check several boxes beyond family needs, the first being facility for entertaining. That limited our choices considerably. We landed on a one-story house at the corner of Cashua and Fairway Drive, the home of Mandeville Rogers, within the Florence Country Club on a four-acre lot. In the front, a horseshoe driveway passed through a substantial brick two-vehicle carport allowing for easy delivery of groceries at the kitchen door. With sliding glass doors, the large open living room circulated onto a larger glassed-in brick porch, together providing ample space for flow and entertaining. The backyard sloped gently down to a two-goal basketball court, not regulation, but sufficient for the many games played there by Walt and neighborhood kids. That group would expand to distant neighborhoods when they got driver's licenses. Beyond the basketball court was an artesian well that fed a quarter-acre pond, full of fish and water moccasins, and past that, the back property line was defined by Jeffries Creek and the swamp around it. There was ample room for parking or outdoor faculty events. There were three bedrooms, two full and one half-bath. A sufficient number of boxes were checked, and the price of $75,000 fit within the budget set for seed money for the college. Rhondda was reasonably satisfied with the place. I could put in a garden past the artesian well, which could provide irrigation, though I had to be vigilant about the snakes. We arrived at our new home on a summer evening in mid-June, 1970.

After our first attempt at arranging the furniture, I turned my attention to the business of the college, specifically marketing.

The legislation creating the college had identified it as Marion State College. At a meeting of the newly constituted board in March, I had made the point that there were already one or two other Marion Colleges in the country and argued that using the full name of the revolutionary war hero would give the new institution a distinctive name, more of an identity. It would be recognized by young students everywhere, but especially by the students in the Pee Dee area of the state, where the general tormented the occupying British forces with guerilla warfare conducted from the local swamps into which his men would vanish. It had only been a few years since the Swamp Fox television series, and there was a series of books. The board agreed, and the legislature concurred. The new school was named Francis Marion College.

It was 1970. Richard Nixon was in the White House and the former Maryland governor was his vice president, at least for a little while. The war in Vietnam raged, and I had two sons, both of whom would be eligible for the draft before the fall of Saigon on April 30, 1975. Not a night passed without news of the war on the evening news. While we were preparing to open our doors for business at FMC, at Kent State University students were protesting the US incursion into Cambodia. Four were shot dead by National Guard troops. Fourteen-year-old runaway Mary Ann Vecchia had been standing beside Jeffrey Miller. In the next moment, a photograph captured her kneeling over Miller's lifeless body. The photo won a Pulitzer Prize for the photographer and became indelibly imprinted in our minds. Neil Young composed "Ohio," condemning the Guard's response to the peaceful protest.

The new college was to begin its official functions on July 1, 1970, which required that the board oversight be transferred from the University of South Carolina board to the state college's board of trustees. Contemporaneously, the state legislature considered an appeal from College of Charleston advocates that effective July 1, 1970 oversight also be transferred from the College of Charleston board to the state colleges board of trustees, chaired by Jim Rogers of Florence. It was approved and transfer ceremonies were scheduled.

In Florence, the ceremony was to begin at noon, allowing for travel time for the board members coming from Charleston. Dr. William Paterson was the provost of the University of South Carolina, and he arrived early. Metal folding chairs had been neatly arranged in front of Stokes Hall, where they broiled in the sun for hours in advance of the event, making them unusable. The provost kindly joined Delores Miller and the new FMC librarian, Mitchel Reames, in moving the chairs inside Stokes Hall. The transfer ceremony was held, and the provost conveyed the deed of the property to the chairman of the new board of trustees.

Francis Marion College founding president, Dr. Walter Douglas Smith, on the balcony of Wallace Hall in 1970.

Much like my challenges at Winthrop, that summer, I was again on the hunt for new faculty before the soon-to-arrive fall semester, as well as other immediately necessary staff among whom were the college business manager, campus engineer, police chief, dean of students, and secretarial and clerical positions. A budget for the next legislative year was pressing. Some of the positions were easily filled with people from USC Florence. Others required a search. We were fortunate in 1970 that more properly trained people were available than the famine I faced in my Winthrop experience.

My workday settled into a nine-to-five routine at the office, followed by dinner at home, after which the dining-room table became my desk to read or prepare paperwork, generally getting a jump on matters to be confronted the following day. The marketing continued. As the first president of the new college, I was regularly called upon to speak to local civic groups and to make frequent appearances on television and radio. I was grateful for these opportunities to pitch the college. Pee Dee-area students needed to know about the new local four-year college on their menu of college choices. It was now a reality. We began with the second summer session of 1970. The curriculum I had prepared some months earlier was implemented, and although there was some apprehension about it, we found that it was accepted by both students and faculty.

Students were generally working toward a four-year degree at FMC, though some anticipated transferring to Carolina or elsewhere. The fall enrollment numbered 907, a 45-percent improvement over the average enrollment of USC Florence of 500. The vision of advocates for a local four-year institution, advancing the goal of bringing into higher education larger numbers of local high-school graduates, was validated. Though the South Carolina Legislature was not generous in budgeting for the new college in its first year, it came through when we asked for money to construct new buildings. Money for a new library and a science building was approved immediately, with the library built and occupied in 1971 and the science building in 1972. Because Jim Rogers was an early supporter of the new school and because he had been a loyal, determined, and effective board chairman, I proposed that his name be placed on the library building. Governor McNair had been the visionary, inspiring the initial studies that led to the founding of the college, and because he had vigorously supported it, I proposed that the science building be named for him. The board agreed to both.

Our plans to this point had not included dormitories. All our students were commuters. The college needed facilities around which a student community could come together. Plans for the third building soon crystalized, and we were able to advance the plans through the board and the legislature. Construction began in 1973, for use in the following year. By locating under one roof the dining facilities, large lounge areas, a basketball court, dressing rooms, handball courts, an art-display area, meeting rooms for clubs and classrooms, the building was unusually functional. and that was our goal for the building and the campus. Incorporating the gymnasium and natatorium into the student center would encourage involvement in intramural athletics. By locating an art gallery in the lounge areas, art was brought into every student's life. Behind the building, the first baseball field was put in as well as fields for soccer and other field sports.

Construction was completed in early 1974, and the student center needed a name. I proposed that it be named not for a single person, but to honor all the many people who had been so supportive in the making of Francis Marion College. The name should be "Founders Hall." As the board deliberated the matter, there was a call for an executive session, which required the two college presidents, Ted Stern of the College of Charleston and me to leave the room. We were barely in the hall before we were invited to return. The matter of naming the building must have been resolved before the meeting was convened. When we again took our seats, it was announced that the building would be named the "Walter Douglas Smith College Center." I was nonplused, pleased, and embarrassed, wondering how this would be received by faculty and staff.

By the time the college center opened, Walt was nearing graduation from West Florence High School, which opened the same year as the college. His high-school years were a success and passed quickly. He played a trumpet in the school bands and was a part of several clubs, including Key Club. Outside of school, he toured North and South Carolina on the Florence YMCA swimming team, worked as a lifeguard at the Florence Country Club and at the FMC pool where he met Pearl Moore. I had hired Sylvia Hatchell to her first college basketball head coaching job. After amassing a 272–80 record at Francis Marion over eleven years, Sylvia became the head coach at the University of North Carolina at Chapel Hill. The Tar

Heel basketball teams became regulars at the NCAA tournament almost immediately as Sylvia reached the rarified air of being among only three women's basketball head coaches to top one thousand career wins. She was rewarded with many awards, including induction into the Hall of Fame. Sylvia stayed in touch with me until her retirement in 2019. At Francis Marion, Pearl did a lot to launch Hatchell's career, averaging 30.6 points per game with a single game record of 60 points, and achieving a college career record of 4,061 points in an era that did not have the three-point arc. She went on to the professional league and was inducted to the Women's Hall of Fame (2011) and the Naismith Memorial Hall of Fame (2021).

Walt pedaled a Lambert 10 speed bicycle down the back roads to FMC and to Darlington, once representing his school on the Darlington Raceway, raising money for a charity. Rhondda drove him to school but only as a freshman. As soon as he had a license, Walt took the wheel of Rhondda's Pontiac Catalina, frequently picking up friends on the way to school.

Ian had been a Phi Beta Kappa graduate from Rice University. When he returned to Florence from the Massachusetts Institute of Technology and Woods Hole Institute, he taught a freshman course in mathematics at FMC, worked on the campus ground crew, and attended classes that resulted in a bachelor of arts degree in psychology. Briefly considering graduate school at Florida State, he decided to become a doctor, studying at the Medical University of South Carolina (MUSC) in Charleston.

RETURN TO AUSTRALIA

In the dining room of our Florence home, a small silk Australian flag waved over an air vent. It had been twenty-seven years since Rhondda had seen her home country. Confident that the college would not collapse in my absence, we decided in 1973 to see what had changed there and what had not. Walt joined us, but Ian was working and unable to miss six weeks for the trip during the Australian summer. Boarding a flight in December from Columbia to San Francisco, we hailed a taxi to take us to the nearby Holiday Inn, where we had visitors. The evening before our morning flight to Nadi, Fiji Islands, Rhondda's brother, Ian, and his wife, Donna Miller, with David and Virginia Compton (David married after Joyce died a couple of years earlier) were able to visit with us.

After a two-hour refueling stop in Honolulu, we were hurling down the runway to Fiji, where we were treated to three days of tropical fruit, lush flower gardens, crystal-clear lagoons, exotic birds, beaches, and snorkeling exploration among tropical fish over coral reefs. On this leg of the trip, Walt was the "pollywog" crossing the equator for the first time. Fiji was enchanting, and the natives were friendly and welcoming, although cannibalism has a long history in Fiji. We returned to the airport. Lifting off, we left the three-hundred-island archipelago of Fiji behind and searched for the Australian coastline in the distant west.

We settled into a comfortable hotel room in the Kings Cross area of Sydney, about six miles from the Miller family home in Vaucluse and a six-minute drive to the Sydney Opera House in the evening shadow of the Sydney Harbor Bridge. We went on tours and visited family, meeting Glenda Wraith, daughter of Rhondda's cousin, as well as Tony and several other cousins in Sydney. Glenda had previously visited us in Rock Hill. By mail, Rhondda had introduced us to the family living at twenty-five Vaucluse Road, providing our projected arrival in the country and a request to visit her former home. Of course, in twenty-seven years, the home had seen many updates that were not familiar to her, including new kitchen cabinets; but looking under the sink, she happily recognized the old-fashioned wallpaper.

A 200-mile south by southwest excursion brought us to the nation's capital of Canberra for a few days, before continuing on that course to Melbourne, about four hundred miles in the same direction at the southernmost mainland point of the country. Cousin Bill and Patti Nielson, and their three sons welcomed us to their city, showing us around. After a few days, we began the return leg of our adventure with a week on the South Island of New Zealand. We had visited the beautiful city of Christchurch and had arrived in Auckland on the north island when Walt began showing symptoms of constant drowsiness and respiratory difficulty at night. A doctor, wearing a suit with Bermuda shorts, came to our hotel room and, after an examination, declared that Walt had contracted mononucleosis, we speculated from the swimming pool in Fiji, bringing our travels to an end four days early. We boarded the next Quanta's flight back to Nadi, Fiji, for a layover at the same hotel from our stay weeks earlier, enjoying dinner and relaxing before a late-night flight to Hawaii and San Francisco. Walt responded well to the medications and had recovered after a few days home in Florence.

Back to Work

In the early years, the college grew rapidly, generally 10 percent to 30 percent each year. New buildings, bigger budgets, new faculty and staff were needed, increasingly putting me in touch with the state leaders of the time. Nurturing these relations would benefit the college. John West succeeded Bob McNair in the South Carolina

Governor's Mansion. He asked me to serve as chairman of a commit-tee on Undergraduate Medical Education as an initial step toward his objective of a second medical school in the state to be located at the University of South Carolina in Columbia. He would succeed in that endeavor. Accepting the responsibility would reward the college with political points.

Neither the Pee Dee area of South Carolina, nor Francis Marion College, ever had much political clout in Columbia. The turnover rate of our members in the house and senate would not allow it. No one built any real seniority, leaving us with no legislators in Columbia who would go to bat and win for the college. Although they were helpful when asked, they never appeared to champion the welfare of the college as one of their primary political goals.

Waiting for legislators to achieve senior roles in the statehouse as a tactic for strengthening our influence in the legislature was a long-game strategy, but the college was burgeoning, and time was not on our side. We courted Spot Mozingo of Hartsville and tar-geted the senior leadership in the statehouse, Senator Edgar Brown and Representative Sol Blatt, both part of the "Barnwell Ring." They were an influential group of South Carolina Democratic legislators from Barnwell County, the four occupying the most powerful posi-tions in state government. Brown and Blatt have their names on large state-government office buildings on the campus of the statehouse. They needed to become friends of Francis Marion College. Jim Rogers and I visited them in their home offices. Rep. Sol Blatt, speaker of the house for many years, seemed delighted to chat with us for two hours, even though he explained he was late for an appointment in Columbia. We then hurried to Senator Brown's office and found him prepared for our meeting. He was the senior South Carolina sena-tor and possessed great influence in the state. The walls of his office were adorned with autographed photographs of himself with various prominent people, including Roosevelt and all the presidents since Roosevelt. After another productive meeting, we again enjoyed the countryside on our way back to Florence, having boosted the voice of the college in Columbia, but it would be short-lived. Mozingo, Blatt, and Brown only lived a few more years.

The fact that Jim Rogers was editor of the *Florence Morning News* opened doors for us, and I was grateful he was the chairman of my board. He was genuinely energized for FMC to achieve its potential. Anecdotally, Jim's style with influential legislators was to shake hands and not let go until he was sure the representative or senator understood why he should get behind FMC causes and how he should vote. Notably, I refer only to the masculine pronoun *he* since a woman would not be elected to the South Carolina State Senate for another thirty-eight years (Katrina Shealy 2012). Nurturing political relationships never ended and continuously evolved with each election cycle.

Frictions between the college and the community were few, but the inevitable decision of the board to build dormitories on campus for the steadily growing student body was not well received by a local real-estate developer, Bill Dailey. He had acquired a tract across Highway 301 from FMC with designs on building student housing. I had assured him at the time that the college had no immediate plans to build residential facilities on campus, and at the time, my opinion was firm but plans change as needs change. Bill then proceeded to purchase modular and stackable apartments bearing no resemblance to the more substantial brick structures he had shown me when I offered that assurance. By comparison, the modular units appeared flimsy, built quickly, and inexpensive. It was not long before students began to complain about the units and about the maintenance Dailey provided. The college took a "hands-off" approach to the dispute between the students and Dailey Development Inc. residential life is important to the institution, and it was apparent that the future of the college could not depend on Bill Dailey for residential facilities. He was not providing adequate services and the college could not afford to allow substandard construction to stall the growth of the institution. On the heels of the decision to build dormitories, Mr. Dailey complained to his lawyer, David Keller, who at that time was a member of the South Carolina House of Representatives.

Keller called and upbraided me for my treatment of Dailey, suggesting that I had not been forthright in my relations with his client. The call was followed with my appearance before a small legislative committee on the funding of the new dorms, and Dailey was present to protest the proposal. He produced my letter to him from five years earlier, in which I indicated that the college did not plan to construct dormitories in the foreseeable future, which he seemed to interpret as binding, though, on its face, it was limited by *foreseeable future*. I explained my position to the committee, and we received the funding and the permission to begin construction. Years later in 1999, Rhondda had a room in a nursing facility. Dailey's mother occupied a room nearby. I had not seen him since the conflict. We talked pleasantly, and the past dispute seemed forgotten. Long after the campus residence halls were built, the college continued to cooperate with him and his housing business.

One other contentious legislative hearing comes to mind. Appearing in support of other proposed buildings for Francis Marion with FMC business manager Casey Frederick at my side, I was verbally assaulted by Senator Roddey of Lancaster, a Winthrop ally. He accused FMC of improper use of funds covering construction expenditures to the exterior of the buildings in the nature of electrical connections, water connections, and landscaping. He bored in relentlessly. I turned to Casey. He was ready with evidence in hand that the senator was in error, that our procedure was both correct and legal. Accordingly, I responded to the senator's charges, and the senator had little more to say. I later learned that while my presentation may have been persuasive, we got the funding because of Senator Jack Lindsay of Bennettsville, the chairman of the committee. He had quieted Senator Roddey and demanded approval of the funding, another illustration of the benefit of having a powerful legislator in the district. Jack Lindsay became a good friend of FMC, but like the others, he died soon after reaching the zenith of his power in the senate.

Walt had considered his choice of colleges after high school, having applied to three, the College of Charleston, Clemson, and on my suggestion, Alabama. All three accepted him for admission. Not surprisingly, the list did not include the college where his father was president, despite my bribes of a car and an apartment. I was scheduled to chair a reaccreditation committee at the University of Alabama in Tuscaloosa, and Walt joined me on my preliminary planning trip, going by way of Clemson with a stop at Birmingham Southern. For two days, Walt was escorted around the Tuscaloosa campus by two daughters of the chairman of the UA accreditation-planning committee. The girls introduced him to the fraternity with which they were affiliated as "little sisters," and he met the director of the Million Dollar Band. In his sophomore year, he would join both. Adding his trumpet to the band gave him a free seat and transportation to the stadiums where the Crimson Tide would play on Saturdays, coached by legendary coach, Paul "Bear" Bryant. Also in that year, he began playing rugby for the university, taking him to various college campuses and other venues in the southeast. After the Seymour sisters showed him around, he was sold on Alabama. Four years later, he would leave Tuscaloosa with a bachelor of arts degree in political science on his way to law school and the practice of law in Columbia. The year 1978 was a big one for the Smith boys. Ian graduated at the top of his class at MUSC. He married Jeanie Simons of Aiken at the Smith College Center and moved to Rochester, New York, for a residency at Strong Memorial Hospital.

Rhondda's days in the seventies were healthy, occupied with the usual housewife responsibilities of the era, supervising Walt, shopping for groceries and other personal needs, preparing dinner, gardening, and the like. Leisure time was spent at the end of a couch in the den by a side table, reading British history and fiction set in British history. On the side table was a glass of beer with ice. There was no second beer as the first would last for hours. She was frequently at my side, attending various social events of the college. Our schedule of weekly dinners, entertaining faculty departments, continued. After we left Winthrop, she never sang in another church choir. She maintained her interest in painting and sculpting and took classes with Jack Dowis at the college. With her own car, she drove herself about town as needed, frequently to the library. We had regular correspondence with Patti Nielsen, the wife of her cousin Bill, in Melbourne. She maintained her own bank account and was as independent as she wished. Rhondda was certainly my intellectual equal, but when we married, I think she looked to me for the larger decisions affecting the family.

Changes came to the board of trustees when Chairman Jim Rogers suffered a heart attack around 1975, requiring his resignation from the position. He was replaced by Mitchell "Cussie" Johnson of Charleston. Jim remained on the board before ultimately resigning entirely and was always a strong voice. Our neighbor, an ophthal-mologist in practice with his sons, Howard Stokes, assumed his seat on the board. Many years earlier, in addressing his Kiwanis Club, Howard had suggested that the Pee Dee area of the state needed a college, and he spearheaded the effort that led to the establishment of the two-year regional USC Florence. Bearing his name, it was from an office in Stokes Hall, where Delores Miller represented the incoming president. Not surprisingly, he was a leader in bringing a four-year college to Florence. Our homes separated by a vacant lot at the time, at the end of the day, Howard and I often shared a drink and our views on world and local affairs. It was on one such evening he suggested that something was needed to draw the community and the college together, that the community should feel invested in the college, and so emerged the idea for the "Sly Fox Club." It was early in 1971, and the college was not well known. The Sly Fox Club would bring together men of the community having an interest in FMC and its activities. We would meet for an hour once per month at the Cherokee Motel dining room for drinks and conversation, but no business. Drinks were fifty cents on the honor system. Bob Ward was the public relations director for Francis Marion, and he would manage the money and pay the bills. Beginning at 6:00 p.m., it was a stand-up affair. After a half hour, Howard, the self-appointed head fox, would call the meeting to order and call for reports from the college. Athletics were a frequent subject of the reports. I would offer a few comments from the administration before Cliff Cormell and others shared jokes. It was an all-male gathering that drew little com-ment at the time. The club continued through my presidency and well into Tom Stanton's years. I credit Howard and the Sly Fox Club for drawing FMC and the community together. Many local business men, lawyers, doctors, and government leaders took part, and it proved to be a great public-relations device.

Despite my background in psychology, I cannot say any special philosophical positions directed my relationships with my sons, who were born five years apart. I delighted in the arrival of each, and when they were infants, I played as big a role in caring for them as I could; however, as they grew into little boys, my job had to dominate my time, and Rhondda carried the greater weight of rearing the boys. We were probably more anxious about the first child, springing into action with Ian's every whimper. Along the way, we learned that every whimper was not a crisis, and the experience informed our care of Walt. At night, as I worked in my study, preparing my lectures for the next day or going over student submissions, the boys were frequently there with me.

In all our travels, the boys went along with us to California to visit their maternal grandparents, "Nana and Pop," Joyce, David and their boys, to Harriman and Rockwood, visiting my family, to Mexico and Europe, we would never have gone to these places without them, even if there were options. In fact, a large part of the reason for these trips was for them to see the country and the world and give them some insight into the cultures and people living in other parts of the world: camels in Morocco, the Trevi fountain and coliseum in Rome, the countryside of Tuscany, the Alps, castles, Piccadilly Circus, the New York World's Fair, pyramided temples in Mexico, and the vast open spaces we saw in our transcontinental travels across this country. Pictures in magazines and books cannot create those memories. It took a world war for me to have that opportunity.

Ian and Walt made their ways through school without any serious challenges. We kept up with what they were studying and their progress, and we talked about school as building toward a goal. We talked about the future: their interests and what they might like to do for a living when the schooling was over. Ian was an only child for five years before his brother arrived, and we probably talked to him as an adult more so than Walt, and as a result, he may have been given more direction. I recall walking around the Winthrop campus with Ian, in front of the music hall, not far from the first house. Ian was about twelve years old and was climbing on the low limbs of a tree when we had one of those conversations. I brought up the field of physics. He was already interested in science and was equipped with a chemistry set, a microscope purchased from the college, and other science-related items. In another ten years, he would leave Houston with a degree in physics. Walt came along when my duties as dean were most demanding, so he did not get the same measure of mature conversation with me about the future.

By the 1960s, my parents and their siblings were well into their twilight years. Many of their siblings had preceded them to the cemetery. Diagnosed with liver cancer, we lost my dad on May 11, 1965. Ten years earlier, he had suffered what must have been a mild heart attack. A week before his passing, I had stopped in Harriman on my way to Texas on college business. He was confined to his bed, but we talked at length. His death occurred shortly after my return to Rock Hill, and I was glad for having made the detour. In Walnut Hill Baptist Church, where my dad was a charter member and declared that no minister would drive him away, I sat in the front pews with other family members; dark sunglasses on to hide my tears, I mourned as I would continue to do for some time. Dad was seventy-three.

Four years later, on April 10, 1969, we lost Mom at the age of seventy-five of uncertain causes, but probably related to injuries sustained in a car crash two years earlier. Riding in the back seat, Vee was driving, and a friend rode up front with her. They were on their way to Knoxville when a young male college student approached from behind and clipped the rear corner of Vee's car as he was attempting to pass, sending it careening into the guard rail. Mom's head must have struck something hard, and she was in critical condition when she entered the hospital in Knoxville. Within minutes of getting the news, I was in the car and on my way. She made a fair recovery, and after a time, she was released, returning to the apartment Benny and Vee had earlier added to their home for her. She was closely monitored by them, and I was in regular contact. Mom's behavior changed, suggesting some brain damage, but she was active for the next two years before deterioration took hold, and she was placed in the Harriman Hospital. She remained there for most of her last year. I visited her on the day she died, but she did not recognize me.

Through the 1970s and into the 1980s, the FMC enrollment swelled to about three thousand by my retirement. New majors and new faculty were added every year. When I lost Hugh Bailey to the presidency of Valdosta State College, I was again on the hunt for a new academic vice president. Dr. William "Bill" C. Moran had served in that position at Berry College in Rome, Georgia, and was at the time working at Winthrop as the arts and sciences dean. We had worked together on a Southern Association of Colleges and Schools committee, and he had earned my appreciation as a knowledge-able and ethical educator with sound judgment and a good sense of humor, all qualities helpful to the position.

To avoid rumors getting started, I met Bill at a restaurant in Lancaster, South Carolina. The same precaution was necessary in 1972 when I met with Bill Grier at a Camden restaurant. He was chairman of the Winthrop board, and we met so he could offer me the presidency at Winthrop. Though I really wanted the job, FMC was still in its formative years, and my conscience would not allow me to accept. At the time I met with Bill Moran (1978), an old friend of mine was president of Winthrop, Charlie Vail, and my conscience hesitated at luring Bill away from Winthrop. I did not want to alien-ate a friend, but we continued to talk, the job was offered, and Bill accepted. He later informed me that Charlie indeed did not take the news well. Charlie was angry for a while but ultimately got over it.

Bill did a brilliant job for Francis Marion. It was my practice to schedule weekly meetings with each vice president and additional meetings as necessary. Bill and I were in synchrony with each other, and it was apparent the vice president of the college and dean of the faculty spoke for the academic program and for the president when I was away. We enjoyed a most compatible working relationship for five years when I retired (1983). I was on the board of Lander College when President Larry Jackson retired, and Bill's name for the vacancy was the first to come to mind. He had been in the running for the position at FMC, but it is difficult to advance to the presidency from within the institution, and he was not offered the job. He was at Lander for eight years.

After taking the bar exam, Walt began dating the girl next door, literally. Their second-floor apartments had connecting backdoors. Mary Ann Edwards was working at a law office as an administrative assistant. They were married on October 9, 1982 at First Baptist Church of Batesburg, and the reception was held in the backyard of her parent's home in Leesville, South Carolina. Ian was his best man. A daughter, Miller, was their firstborn on May 29, 1987, and was given Rhondda's maiden name, which delighted her. Their son, Hayden, followed on January 29, 1993. With Ian and his family in Lancaster, Pennsylvania, working in a large cardiology practice, we enjoyed having Walt and his family only an hour and twenty minutes away in the Forest Acres part of Columbia, where we could visit regularly.

We did visit in Rochester, New York, during Ian's residency at Strong Memorial, but never later than November and never earlier than the snow had melted. Winters there were brutal, so it took a few months for us to meet our granddaughter, Loren, after her birth on January 30, 1980. They had purchased a house in an old Rochester neighborhood. We were back in Rochester to help them pack and move to Durham for Ian's fellowship in cardiology at Duke University. Ian drove a rental truck, and Jeanie drove their car, both stuffed with their belongings. We had a layover at the home of a Simon's family member in a small town in New York to introduce Loren, who tolerated travel well, perhaps foreshadowing her extensive travel in the future.

It was not long before Loren would have a little brother. Brewster was born on February 11, 1983. He was only a few months old when Ian completed the Durham fellowship, and they were again packing for the move to Lancaster, Pennsylvania, where Ian would join a group of five physicians in a cardiology practice. Rhondda, Walt, and I contributed to the move, pulling a trailer full of plants. In future years, Rhondda and I made that trip a couple of times a year, sometimes to watch over their children while Ian and Jeanie got away. It gave us a chance to meddle in their lives the way grandparents do instinctively. We were there when Brewster was a patient at the Will Eye Institute for minor surgery and when Ian was a patient at the University of Pennsylvania Hospital for a rheumatic issue. The opportunities to be with Loren and Brewster created enduring memories for us and them.

After living in Lancaster, Pennsylvania, for fifteen years, Ian and Jeanie decided it was time for their return to the south. The subject came up increasingly over the years until the summer of 1997. I was spending a week on the Chesapeake with both of my sons on a thirty-foot sailboat. We had gone ashore in a small bayside village for breakfast when the subject came up again. He had been offered a position with advanced cardiology associates in Florence. To crystalize the decision to be made, I wrote down a dozen factors to be considered, handed the paper to Ian, and asked him to rate each, 0 to 5 for staying in Lancaster or moving to Florence. Ian applied his rating to each factor, added the scores, and Florence emerged as the clear winner. "Well, I guess we are moving to Florence," he concluded. After another day of sailing, Walt and I returned to Florence, pleased that Ian and family would be back in South Carolina. By the following summer, they had settled into a nice home zoned for nearby West Florence High School.

When Ian's family moved to Florence in 1998, Loren took a "gap year" before starting her freshman year at the University of Maryland—visiting Arizona, Mexico, Australia, and New Hampshire. In May 2000, I was in College Park, Maryland, to see her. With Loren driving, we took a white knuckle trip into downtown Washington, where we ate at an Indian restaurant and visited a museum. At one point, we found ourselves in the middle of a gay pride parade! We enjoyed the time together, socking away more fond memories for us. After her first year at Maryland, Loren transferred to Macalester College in St. Paul, Minnesota. She was always a good student.

Brewster finished high school at West Florence, where his uncle Walt had graduated, and decided on Clemson for his college education. Though he had a strong background in computer science, that may have been too narrow a focus. He opted for a major in engineering while at the same time considering a future in medicine. Loren and Brewster are intelligent, healthy, and strong, but not impervious to poor decisions; and as their grandfather, I am vigilant about how they navigate life. Lack of control is the engine driving the worry of a grandparent.

As I write this, Miller and Hayden are still in their formative years. At age fourteen, Miller is an active freshman at Cardinal Newman School, performing in school-stage productions and playing softball for the school, and Hayden is a fourth grader, playing baseball at Trenholm Little League, not far from their home. Walt and Mary Ann are very much engaged in everything their children do, including coaching. I only get to see them about once a month, but we are on the phone together almost daily.

It was in 1983 that I considered retirement from FMC, not because I felt old or no longer up to the challenges. I was in good mental and physical health. After thirty years in college and university work, I had done everything once, and some things too many times to be interested in doing them again. I had well exceeded the number of service years necessary to receive full retirement benefits, and any disparity between employment income and retirement income would be nominal. I was sixty-five, and I needed a new challenge. After a few thoughtful weeks and conversations with the State Retirement System and Rhondda, the decision was made, and I announced my retirement to the board of trustees, effective July 1, 1983. Four months later, Rhondda and I were rewarded by the FMC faculty with a trip to Spain, Portugal, and Morocco. It was the best traveling experience of our lives. Flying into Madrid, we toured the surroundings before setting out for Toledo, Cordoba, Malaga, Algeciras, Tangiers, Seville, Lisbon, and back to Madrid on an escorted tour that was informative and relaxing. The weather throughout our journey was clear and beautiful, and when it was over, we came home to decide what was next.

My retirement announcement was made well in advance of the effective date. There was much to do, to disengage as the college president and to map a seamless transition for the college's second president. Mrs. Helen DesChamps, the mother-in-law of my friend,

Bill Blackwell, and our across-the-street neighbor in Country Club Estates, wanted to sell her house, making the move to the Presbyterian retirement home. We took a tour of the house and found the size and location suitable to our needs. It was forty-three years old, with timbers far more substantial than those employed in new construction. The wiring and plumbing were old and would require replacement at some point, but it was comfortable. Sitting on a double lot, the yard was full of camellias and other flowering plants, and it had a nice space by the garage for my garden.

Located across the street was Timrod Park, an eighteen-acre recreational area named for Henry Timrod, a teacher whose one room (twelve feet by fifteen feet) schoolhouse was moved there to be preserved. A second generation American of German descent, Timrod was a poet, like his father. His studies at the University of Georgia were cut short by illness, and he returned to the family home in Charleston with designs on practicing law, which, by December of 1850, he had determined was "distasteful." He continued writing and publishing his poems until 1856, when he accepted a teaching position on the plantation of William Henry Cannon, a part of which became Florence. I could imagine daily walks through the park and indeed that became my routine.

The Graham Street house had been built by Helen DesChamps and her first husband in 1939. Rhondda wanted to build a new home and spent considerable time drawing floor plans, but we ultimately decided on the DesChamps house. A week prior to Christmas, 1982, Rhondda and I moved to 609 South Graham Street, a federalist style two-story house also across the street from the old Florence Museum at the edge of the park. We did not know at the time that Rhondda would one day occupy a room at the nursing home two blocks away.

With money realized on the sale of our house at 724 Fairway Drive, renovations began on antebellum-styled Wallace Hall for the incoming president, a process I hurried along because the beautiful home might be a carrot to attract the new leader of the school.

THE GOVERNOR'S SCHOOL FOR SCIENCE AND MATHEMATICS

It was 1984, and Coker College in Hartsville, South Carolina, was in trouble. Unable to compete with less expensive state-supported colleges, including Francis Marion only thirty miles away, enrollment was on a steady decline, and it appeared the school was in its last months of operation. Coker seemed overwhelmed by the times. The intimacy of the small college atmosphere may have also lost its appeal to the new crop of local high school graduates. Jim Rogers had become the chairman of the Coker board and reached out to various religious institutions—Baptists, Episcopalians, and others— but they all had too many colleges, more than they could support. I was in regular conversation with Jim and well aware of the problems in Hartsville. For some time, I had watched the growth and success of the North Carolina School for Mathematics and Science in Durham, North Carolina, a public residential high school, serving students from across the state, studying a specialized curriculum of science and mathematics, but also offering courses in the humanities. Established in 1978, by 1984, it had matured and could provide the model for a similar school in this state to be housed at Coker. I had long believed that the academic upper tier of students in South Carolina were underserved, and that the state should make a special effort to provide the best possible education for them. With the lessons learned from our experiences in starting Francis Marion and the credentials and clout earned in Columbia, we determined to combine two purposes, providing an enhanced education to South Carolina's best and brightest and to create an income stream from the state to Coker. We were not sure how that second purpose would work and what exactly the relationship between the college and state would look like.

Jim took the idea to Dr. Jim Daniels, president of Coker College, who had been watching the ship go down. With fewer students, Coker needed fewer faculty and staff, and the demise of the school accelerated. Dr. Daniels was very receptive, and a follow-up meeting was scheduled at the home of Mrs. Julian Price Jr., another Coker board member, and I was asked to expound on my idea. As we collaborated, I was informed that Dr. James B. Holderman, president of the University of South Carolina was trying to sell the Coker board on giving the Coker facilities to USC for the establishment of a justice center. Of course, the university would also acquire the Coker endowment worth millions of dollars. The ever-tenacious Jim Rogers went to work on his board, convincing a majority to go with my plan to establish a math and science school on the Coker campus. Later, I was told by Jim Daniels that when the board asked that Jim Rogers chair the committee to pursue the plan, he consented on the condition that I serve as cochairman. When asked what made him think I would also consent, Jim replied, "I'll see that he serves." Jim knew me well. In fact, he told me that I was asked to serve as the chairman, rather than cochairman, and he deferred to me in heading up committee meetings. In less than ten years, Dr. James B. Holderman would resign from USC amid financial and sexual scandals, going to prison after pleading guilty to income tax evasion. It was a long fall for a man who held celebrity status in the state. About a decade later, he was arrested again by the FBI, whose agents posed as Russian mobsters. He returned to prison for scheming to launder drug money.

The first order of business for the committee was to schedule a visit to the North Carolina school. All the committee members made the trip to Durham and the shuttered Watts Hospital, where the school was housed. When we talked about the kind of school to be created, it was always assumed that it would be situated on the Coker campus, but we did not try to define its relationship with the college—that is, would it be a subsidiary of Coker or would it operate independently. The answer was linked to its funding by the state. The new school would need to be organized as an agency of the state and function in that way.

The planning committee made many trips to Columbia for consultations with Governor Dick Riley before the expiration of his term at the end of the year, and then with Governor Carroll Campbell in the new term. We learned that Speaker Pro Tem Jack Rogers of Bennettsville, representative David Beasley, chairman of the House Education committee, and Senator Jack Lindsay, also of Bennettsville were all very supportive. Curiously, Charlie Williams, the state superintendent of education, opposed the school. However, with the support of the governor and these legislators, his objections were silenced.

As the bill made its way through the legislature, attention was given to naming the school. One I thought had merit was the "McNair-Townes School for Science and Mathematics." Ron McNair was the South Carolina-born astronaut who died when NASA's Challenger space shuttle on its tenth flight exploded and broke apart seventy-three seconds after launching. Like learning about the assassination of President Kennedy or about the 9-11 attacks, it was a seminal moment that people tend to remember where they were at the time. Charles Townes was the Furman University-trained native of Greenville, South Carolina, a physicist who created and patented the maser, precursor to the laser, winning the Nobel Prize in physics, and many other awards. Both are well recognized among scientists and citizens of the state, and both were deserving of the honor. Later, the "Charles H. Townes Award" would be the climax of an annual awards dinner for people who had contributed to the success of the school. Accompanied by Walt, I accepted that honor at the annual event in Columbia. Ultimately, word came down from the governor's office that the school would be named "The Governor's School for Science and Mathematics (GSSM)," consistent with the summer programs housed at Furman University and the College of Charleston, both referred to as "Governor's Schools." As a committee, we were not greatly concerned with the name and accepted it without comment. We had worked hard to bring the idea to fruition, and now we had legislative approval and funding.

Following the template for South Carolina colleges and universities, Governor Campbell soon appointed a board of trustees for the GSSM, filling the positions on the board with people having various degrees of influence in the state, including Jim Rogers. The acting provost of USC was appointed chairman of the board. The legislation provided a two-hundred-thousand-dollar budget for the 1985 to 1986 school year, placed the physical location of the school on the Coker campus and called for the first class of eleventh graders to enter in autumn of 1986. However, still unaddressed were details defining the relationship between GSSM and Coker College.

The GSSM board met in July, August, and September of 1985, but without making concrete plans to build the new school. Before the September meeting, Jim told me about the board's actions and lack of accomplishments. He was fully aware that only ten months remained before sixty high-school juniors would show up for classes. Jim must have relayed our conversation to the board in the September meeting, and the board was suddenly aware of the urgency that attended their mission. After some discussion, it was resolved that Jim should ask me to "put the school together." I had put together a four-year college on relatively short notice. My health was good, and I was not busy. Two years after Rhondda and I had returned from the Iberian Peninsula, I had found what I would do next. I accepted the challenge.

On the campus of Northwestern State University, a school for bright high-school juniors and seniors had been established in Natchitoches, Louisiana, the Louisiana School for Math, Science, and the Arts (LSMSA), and a visit to that school was a priority. It would offer more lessons for our mission than the school in Durham. Neither school was under the auspices of the state department of education. Our training standards would be more rigorous with most professors holding PhDs in their field. The administration and structure of our school would resemble a college, and although GSSM graduates would be required to meet the state standards imposed on high-school students across the state, their courses would be structured like college courses, and their weekly activities looked like those of college students.

Before long, the task before me coalesced into a plan. Jim Daniels found a room for me in the administration building at Coker, and I hired a previously retired woman who drove to the campus from nearby Darlington. We were set on our end. Procurement was the next challenge.

I had worked in state government for thirty years and was well acquainted with the procedures for ordering supplies, submitting travel records, and all the other details of procurement, but the young staff of the new governor, Carroll Campbell, was handicapped by inexperience. It is inevitable with every change of administration. The learning curve was about six months, and I did not have six months. They seemed afraid to make a mistake, so they did nothing. Even minor issues stalled our progress. The ordering of a typewriter took weeks to go through. Exasperated, I began to wonder if a sinister figure was behind the intractability of the governor's staff, a figure determined to kill the school before it started, or was the new staff simply that incompetent. I decided to inform the governor of the matter and turned to Jim Rogers. A member of the GSSM board having the ear of the governor needed to remove all obstacles to our mission to start this school. After that, the governor's staff was falling over each other to see that I had everything I needed.

For eight months, Monday through Friday, I drove to Hartsville, first designing the curriculum for the exceptional eleventh and twelfth graders. It had to meet all the state requirements for graduation, and it had to be challenging to the students. The curriculum should be delivered in a way that the students could address the subjects in their own imaginative ways. It had to be more than a lecture given by the professor each day. My job was to conceive and construct the framework of study.

From that framework, there was a lot of writing to be done, manuals for students to describe all aspects of life on campus, including the rules, regulations, and decorum expected of a GSSM student, and similarly, a manual for faculty that described expectations of them. Then, there were the brochures and marketing materials to be used in student recruitment, the most daunting of the tasks before me, but I had a plan.

I called on the education professionals I had met along the way, a dream team of former deans, superintendents, and other retired educators who knew every corner of the state. Their mission: to locate and interview applicants in the counties assigned to them. The plan was a hasty one, but it worked, and by May 1, 1986, their efforts netted sixty-five very intelligent students from all over South Carolina.

There was still the matter of defining the relationship between Coker and GSSM. It was a unique issue never before addressed by the state. I worked and debated the matter with the Coker President and its business manager, and we settled upon a plan that worked well for both schools. The students were only required to pay for their personal expenses, clothes, transportation, incidentals, and the like. The state would pay their tuition and for everything else. The GSSM students would be housed in the largely vacant Coker dormitories, eat at the college cafeteria, and use the Coker libraries and classrooms. For all this, the college would be compensated by the state and serve as an enduring investment in education.

With sixty-five students arriving for classes in less than four months, we needed faculty to teach them, staff to run the school, and a GSSM director. They would all need time to make arrangements, resigning from jobs, finding housing in some cases, making the move, and preparing to teach sixty-five challenging students. Time was in short supply. Lee Cox was the director of the South Carolina committee for the humanities. I had chaired that committee for two years in the seventies and knew Lee quite well. Although his PhD was in English, he had done a masterful job as director and would do the same as the GSSM president. He accepted the position and went to work at the school on May 1, 1986, and I went home, retired again.

THE FLORENCE CHAMBER
OF COMMERCE

The newly elected chairman of the Florence Chamber of Commerce in 1986 was Bryan Jackson, who came to the position with an unexpected dilemma. The Chamber director had left the position with little notice. Bryan asked me to fill in temporarily while the Chamber conducted a search for a permanent director. I knew Bryan as a hard-working entrepreneur and the principal owner of Superior Manufacturing in Florence, purchasing the company some fifteen years earlier. Filling positions was something I had done many times in my career, and I sympathized with him. Again, I had time on my hands and thought I might enjoy the job. I accepted but declined any compensation. I did not want the board to think I had a boss. For five months, I walked the four blocks from my house on Graham Street, working nine to five at the Chamber office, until a new director was hired. I learned about the role of the Chamber in the community and how it was structured to serve that role. With yearly changes to the leadership by annual elections of officers, the organization depended heavily on the reliability and stability of the staff. Bryan and the young and ambitious community leaders were fun collaborators.

As the director, I set about finding my replacement. He was in Oxford, Mississippi. Doug Everett was the director of the Oxford Chamber. He had been recommended by another old friend, the president of the University of Mississippi in Oxford. I communicated the information to the Chamber board; they offered him the position, and again, I was out of a job. I received no W-2 form and no form 1099, receiving instead a lifetime membership in the Chamber.

My work with the Southern Association of Colleges and Schools (SACS) was also unpaid. My affiliation with SACS began after my arrival at Winthrop in 1959, and it continued for five years after retirement in 1988, when I reached age seventy. My name was then purged from their list of prospective committee members. Once or twice a year, the work entailed visiting various colleges and universities across the south to assess the institutions readiness for reaccreditation, with a committee I usually chaired. I enjoyed the work, and in my last few years of service to the organization, I was often asked to visit three or four institutions a year, committing twenty-eight to thirty days away from home in states from Florida to Texas and as far north as Kentucky and Virginia.

IS THIS RETIREMENT?

After retirement from Francis Marion, I got a call from Dr. Kenneth Orr, president of Presbyterian College in Clinton, South Carolina, soliciting my service on his board of trustees, which I accepted, remaining on the board for nine years. In this same time frame, the legislature voted to remove Francis Marion, the College of Charleston, and Lander University from the supervision of the state board of trustees, in favor of each school having their own board. Having worked with Larry Jackson, president of Lander, and counting him as a colleague and friend, I ran for one of the two vacancies in the Lander board in the Sixth Congressional District. I was elected in 1988 and served consecutive four-year terms until 2004, deciding then that it was time for a younger person to fill that role.

When Dr. Lorin Mason vacated his seat on the Francis Marion University Foundation board to take a seat on the FMU board of trustees, he called me about the Foundation and the position of chairman. I accepted and chaired the Foundation from 1989 to 1992 during the presidency of Tom Stanton. Working in the shadow of the founding president might have been awkward for Tom, so I viewed the position as temporary, persuading Dr. Robert Moore, an FMC graduate from the early years and a local orthopedic surgeon, to become the chairman. I resigned from the Foundation, retired, but for the Lander board.

Over my years of college and university work, I held a variety of local and state positions that could be best described as community service, to include the following:

- Two years as chairman of the South Carolina committee for the Humanities
- Two years as chairman of the Florence United Way Board
- Two years as chairman of the Pee Dee Area Boy Scout Council
- One year, while at Winthrop, as president of the South Carolina Psychological Association
- Chairman of one of Governor West's Committees on undergraduate medical education in preparation for the second medical school in the state
- President of the Florence Rotary Club
- President of a South Carolina Legislative committee, studying the twelfth grade in South Carolina public schools
- Temporary director and member of the Florence Chamber of Commerce
- Six years as a member of the SP&L Employees Scholarship Selection committee
- Membership on the Advisory committee of the Florence mayor
- Chairman of the Mayor's Search committee for a new police chief
- Vice president of the Rock Hill Kiwanis Club
- And many other positions that don't readily come to mind.

Over the years, from Tallahassee to Florence, dozens of speeches were delivered to high schools, colleges, universities, churches, service organizations, dedication ceremonies, and other venues. I was the best man at Jack Baker's wedding to Alice. Along with Tom Sills, I delivered the eulogy at the funeral of Charlie Davis. I presented a couple of papers to psychology professional associations and was published in professional journals while a professor at Florida State.

While my range of daily activities diminished after retirement, I found ways to be useful and to be relevant in the lives of my family and in my community. I was never bored. For a while, I felt some guilt to be reading my second newspaper of the day while drinking my second cup of coffee at nine in the morning. But after a time, that went away, and I enjoyed a day with nothing on the calendar.

Rhondda was every bit the model housewife of our generation, always supportive of me and the boys, content in managing the house and the family, singing in the choir, and practicing her talents in the arts. As typically runs concurrent with aging, our social life diminished with each passing year. As the years slipped by, her interests in the matters that had occupied her days diminished, along with her confidence. In the past, I was comfortable leaving Rhondda at home while I was away, but I began to notice changes in her cognition. Her memory had always been keener than mine, but increasingly, she came to me for memories of events. Worrisome things occurred around the house, like forgetting to turn off burners on the stove. It occurred to me that she was showing the same symptoms of Alzheimer's, the progressive disease that had taken her mother.

In the late 1980s, renovations to the Florence Mall were being made, and planks of plywood were laid as pathways from store to store. Rhondda was at the entrance to Belk's when she tripped and took a hard fall. I was called and, with the help of a Belk employee, lifted her to her feet and placed her in the front seat of my car. She declared with certainty that she had broken her left hip. I took her directly to the orthopedic surgeon's office, where her self-diagnosis was confirmed. Dr. Dewey Ervin replaced her hip, and she remained in the hospital for five or six days. With the support of crutches, she was immediately able to ascend the stairs, and she did not undergo any rehabilitation. Recovery was quick, and she was soon driving and functioning as she had before the accident. But there were falls in the aftermath, and she was persuaded to use a walking stick. She was rarely seen without it in her later years. While she was getting along physically, her mental decline became more pronounced, and I became more watchful and protective.

Debbie Bailey, daughter of Hugh and Joan Bailey, married Mark Helwig in November of 1992, and we were on our way to Valdosta, where Hugh was president of Valdosta State. I pulled into a rest area near Savannah, and Rhondda elected to wait in the car. In less than five minutes, I had returned to the car. She was in her seat, but the door was open. She explained that she had fallen in the parking lot and that her right hip was broken. Examining her, it was apparent that there was an injury. She declined consulting a doctor in Savannah, and we returned to Florence, going directly to the emergency room at McLeod Hospital. She submitted to an X-ray. This time, it did not agree with her self-diagnosis, and the doctor pronounced the injury to be a bruise, but not a break.

We went home. Rhondda struggled up the stairs to the bedroom, where she remained in her bed except for trips to the bathroom. Walking was painful, and we improvised, carrying her on a dolly back and forth. After two days, it was apparent that she had more than a bruise, and I called the nurse for Dr. Lorin Mason, who told me to bring her in. I called an ambulance. She was examined by Dr. Cecil Bozard, who declared her hip to be broken. Rhondda was taken to Bruce Hospital, and the following morning, she was on the operating table, and Dr. Bozard was at work on her hip.

Following surgery, she did not return to her room as the doctor had explained and led me to expect. After an hour or so, I asked a nurse to find out what was happening. She advised that Rhondda was agitated, and they were waiting for her to calm. After a while, she was rolled into her room, wrists tied to the railing, in a white hot rage. "Look what they've done to me! Get these things off! Let me out of here!" I asked the nurse to remove the restraints and went about getting her settled.

"Emergence agitation" is not an uncommon phenomenon occurring in the early stages of recovery from anesthesia, and Rhondda experienced all the symptoms, confusion, disorientation, and violent behavior. The concern was that in her thrashing about, she would dislodge the wedge between her legs and upset the hip replacement. I was with her constantly for the next five days to keep that from happening. She was confused and beyond reasoning, and keeping her peaceful was a contest. At night, I was in the recliner beside her, and I assisted in getting her to the bathroom. In time, she was moved to the Bruce Rehabilitation Center for five days. Her confusion slowly abated, but I continued to stay by her side. The confusion predictably returned when she woke. Part of the rehabilitation involved psychological testing because the neurologist had advanced the idea that she was impaired by Alzheimer's disease; however, the psychologist's tests given several times while in the unit did not support that conclusion, and I was left to think that the neurologist may have reached a hasty diagnosis, but he planted a seed.

Rhondda was finally discharged. It was in late 1992. We returned to our Graham Street home, and she resumed living out her normal: driving, shopping, cooking, and reading. Her ability to recall past events was failing, and her emotions were sometimes inappropriate to the events occurring around her. Her expression of love, hate, despair, or anger was flat or absent. Perceptive only to me, her condition deteriorated every day, and the need to be watchful grew in equal measure, particularly with activities to which any level of danger attached. After eighteen months of witnessing her decline and mental retreat, we made an appointment with a local neurologist, another Australian in Florence, Dr. Ashley Kent, and Rhondda was subjected to a battery of tests designed to confirm the Alzheimer's diagnosis he offered a year and a half earlier at Bruce Rehab. It was confirmed. Rhondda was issued a prescription for Cognex, with the hopes of holding the disease in abeyance for three of four years.

Rhondda was strangely without curiosity about the psychological testing and the doctor's conclusions. I just told her the Cognex was to help with her memory. I never used the word "Alzheimer's." She never pressed the matter. She never asked for more detailed information. By mid-1994, I had taken over all the cooking and housework and devoted more and more attention to the details of her life.

Until 1996, life resembled normal, to the extent that Rhondda was still eating, sleeping, and reading, though I suspect her reading retention was waning. We did manage to take short trips to see Walt and his family, which, in that year, included our three-year-old grandson, Hayden. We also managed a family reunion at Watts Bar Lake, where my nephew Gerald had a lake house, south of Rockwood and Harriman. Walt was with us, and together, we monitored her carefully. It would be the last reunion for Rhondda.

By that time, I was assisting Rhondda with her bathing, primarily owing to the risk of her falling. It was the risk I most assiduously guarded against, getting me up at night to take her to the bathroom. She could still use a walker, but would she remember? Help with dressing was next. By the end of 1996, she was completely dependent on my care—bathing and other bathroom visits, cooking, preparing her plate and placing it in front of her, handling her medications, and always avoiding falls. But still, she fell often, and she was unable to assist me in getting her to her feet. One fall from her bed resulted in a gash above her eye that required stitches. Her knees were often bruised.

In those years, Rhondda would often ask me about her family, usually at night before bed. I would explain that her sister, Joyce, and her parents were deceased and that she had attended their funerals. In a half hour, she might ask the same question again. My explanations were sometimes followed by sobbing. "They've died, and I didn't even know about it." In time, the questions were no longer asked.

That time was also attended by her frequent urinary tract infections. Her eating moderated to the point she dropped to 110 pounds from 125. Her dependence on me was complete. She might determine to visit the bathroom twenty times a night, and ever vigilant about the risk of a fall, I would go with her. Sometimes she complained, "I've been caring for myself for fifty years. I think I can do it now." Eventually her protests ended, and I helped her without objection. We were both exhausted. Finally, I hired Leola Brown to care for Rhondda during the day, allowing me to attend to all the tasks that caring for my wife kept me from doing.

In December, my knees were in bad shape. Having Leola at the house also allowed me to visit the orthopedist. I needed a knee replacement, and without it, I would be unable to care for Rhondda or myself. Thankful for my sisters, Jean, Ona, and Glenna made the trip over from Tennessee, and it was my turn on the operating table on December 10, 1996. I occupied a hospital bed for five days before being moved to the rehab center for six days. Soon after I was discharged before Christmas, Ona and Glenna returned to Tennessee, and Jean stayed until after the New Year.

For several weeks, I got around with the help of a walker, then with a cane for another two months, but my knee was too weak for me to give Rhondda the care she required. Heritage Nursing Home on Worley Street was two blocks from the house. I asked about a room for Rhondda. I was not sure if she would only be there until my knee healed or if this was for the duration. There was a private room available, and on January 3, she became a resident. In an effort to simulate her environment at home, a television was placed in the room for the "white noise" it provided, along with some of her paintings and other familiar items. It was a new phase in caring for Rhondda.

She was restless there. Her wits were sufficiently sharp to complain about those "odd people" with whom she dined at a table surrounded by five or six people, all with some degree of dementia, some advanced. Rhondda recognized the dementia in others, but not in herself. Unable to lie quietly in bed or relax in a wheelchair, she wanted to move about the facility. I once entered her wing to see her walking behind her wheelchair. Had I not witnessed this, I might not have made the decision to bring her home for a few days, a trial period to see how we managed, after only three weeks at Heritage. Weighing the risk of falling at Heritage against the risk of falling at home, it seemed best, though my decision to retain the room reflected my level of confidence. Not yet healed, my knee made me understand I was not yet up to resuming full-time care of my wife. I put her in the car, and we drove the two blocks to the nursing home, but when we pulled into the parking lot, she sat stubbornly in her seat, motionless. I drove us home. I would find more help and a way to make it work.

I called Mary Cooper and Thelma Scott, both retired Francis Marion employees and a shift schedule divided supervision responsibility in thirds. Rhondda slept in the first floor-paneled den with Mary sleeping in the recliner beside her from midnight to 8:00 a.m., when Thelma arrived for the next shift until 4:00 p.m. That is when my shift began. It worked well.

A specialized Alzheimer's facility was scheduled to open in Chapin, South Carolina. The Lowman Home was owned by the Lutheran Church and was set to open on March 1, 1997. About twenty-five miles from his home, Walt made the initial inquiries with a visit to the facility and reported his findings. Rhondda was accepted as a resident. Like the families of Alzheimer's patients everywhere, we were looking for a solution. It seemed to offer Rhondda the promise of safety in a pleasant environment. Walt and I delivered her to the facility on opening day. Reasoning that Rhondda would be less suspicious of Walt and more likely to be accepting, he escorted her in, made the introductions to the staff, and settled her in her room. I remained in the car initially. The facility had an open common area, and the halls ends were rounded. Her room was bright and airy, with a partition separating her from her neighbor. Rhondda seemed agreeable to the place. We transitioned to another phase of caring for her.

The Lowman staff seemed to know what they were doing. We were assured that someone would look in on Rhondda every fifteen minutes at night. Nocturnal wandering is a behavior associated with the disease. During the day, she would join others in the common area, in chairs and wheelchairs, and dine with others at tables set for four, with staff close at hand to assist with meals, but also to referee any conflicts between the residents. Angry outbursts and physical aggression are also hallmarks of Alzheimer's. The new arrangement seemed to be working. I visited three times a week, usually around lunch so I could eat with her, and I would leave around midafternoon. Driving ninety miles in each direction, my visits took up most of the day, leading me to consider selling the Florence house and purchasing a house or condominium in closer proximity. I dedicated hours to looking, but the arrangement with Loman I hoped would be the answer began to sour. The staff began reporting falling incidents but with no serious injury. On one occasion, I entered the wide commons area to find Rhondda on the floor, surrounded by staff. On another, the staff called Walt at his office, advising that she had fallen and was on her way to the hospital in Lexington for

X-rays. Walt was at the hospital within twenty minutes of the fall. Facial bruising and swelling made her barely recognizable. Rhondda seemed unable to escape frequent falls, planting seeds of doubt in the ability of Lowman to care for her. By this time, it should have been apparent that this patient presented a higher risk to be guarded against. The tipping point came in late April, some eight weeks after her arrival at Lowman.

An early morning call from Lowman alerted me to yet another fall, this one occurring in the night. It was speculated that she had gotten out of bed. They found her on the floor. I got in the car and drove the ninety miles to the Lowman home and met with the unit director and a nurse. There was an enormous lump on Rhondda's forehead, near her right eye. She was confused and was not talking. I directed that she should be transported to Lexington Medical Center, some twenty-five miles away. She was examined and subjected to another set of X-rays. No serious injury was detected. Two days passed, and she was still not talking or walking, and I again directed that she be seen again at the hospital. After all, I had seen X-rays fail to detect her broken hip. Again, the results were not revealing. She was returned to Lowman. She sat silently in her wheelchair and did not react to anyone.

The Alzheimer's nurse called to ask that I meet with her on my next visit to Lowman. She advised that Rhondda's condition had deteriorated beyond the care available at the Alzheimer's unit, and that she should be transferred to the Lowman Nursing Home. I was in no position to argue but would be quick about making alternative arrangements. Rhondda was in the nursing unit at Lowman for one week before I returned to bring her back to Florence. She was placed in the front passenger seat for the trip directly to the Heritage. She was silent for the entire ninety miles. I was angry with Lowman. They had failed in their pledge of vigilance, particularly at night, and that failure had contributed to Rhondda's deeper retreat into silence. Their abrupt insistence on moving her to the nursing unit was a naked admission. They were incapable of providing the care they assured. A demonstrated lack of compassion for their patient followed. There were no calls from Lowman inquiring about her welfare. For two to three months, Rhondda wore the disfiguring bruise on her forehead. Her cognitive abilities stood in sharp contrast to before the fall, when she could talk and walk. There was little evidence of what she was thinking or if she was thinking at all.

This was the last phase of her care and the last chapter in Rhondda's life. From her admission to the Heritage on May 1, 1997 until her passing on January 7, 2000, the Heritage was her quiet world, other than frequent hospital admissions during her last year. Her bruised forehead settled from a lump into a yellow-and-blue reminder of her fall. Life was simple. Outside the doorway to her room during the day, she joined other patients quietly posted in the hallway like wheelchair-bound sentries, marginally aware of the activity around them. At night, they put her in bed between 7:00 p.m. and 8:0 p.m. Sometimes a nurse would report, "Mrs. Smith spoke to me today. I didn't know she could talk." Though somewhat uplifting, those reports were infrequent and finally ended.

I arrived at the Heritage at 5:00 p.m. daily, spending the first twenty minutes exercising her arms and legs to avoid atrophy and promote flexibility. After her workout, we joined the others in the dining room for dinner. If the weather was good, dinner was followed by sitting outside on the patio until 7:30 or 8:00 p.m. I carried the conversation then rolled her back inside. I left at 8:00 p.m. and allowed the staff to get her into bed. She followed me with her eyes when I left, but made no show of protest.

For the first eighteen months of her second stay at the Heritage, she could give me some response when I talked to her, and when I would bend over her on the bed to give her a goodnight kiss, she would pucker her lips and grin at me. In the last year there, I got very little response, though I assume there was some recognition if only because she saw me for several hours daily.

The home suffered high turnover. It takes a special person to care for special-needs patients, including those suffering dementia, and not every aide was a special person. Some were plainly unfeeling toward their charges. Maybe that is a defense mechanism necessary to the depressing but necessary work. It was my prayer that I stay healthy enough to care for her, and that her needs would not be left to the nursing home staff.

There were techniques to the job. When it was time for me to go home, I pushed the button to summon a nurse. When they did not arrive in a timely fashion, I lifted Rhondda from her chair to the bed, testing the limits of my new knee. I learned how to keep her clean and how to brush her teeth. Our family dentist, Carroll Player, taught me to stand behind her. In fact, I mastered all the skills of a nursing-home aid and practiced them on Rhondda every day, because nursing home care is never adequate, the patients are too many, and the aids are too few because the pay is too little. The patients, having no family to take up the slack, suffer for it. There were some aides with hearts of gold, but more were needed.

Colds seemed epidemic in the Heritage Home in December of 1999, and I kept Rhondda in her room. No doubt, the attendants going room to room did their share to spread the virus adding to the respiratory struggles of many of the elderly residents. My attempt to isolate Rhondda failed. She developed a significant fever and was transported to Carolinas Hospital. Early each morning, I arrived to feed her breakfast, coming back for lunch and for dinner. Eventually, she stopped eating altogether and was dependent on the feeding tubes. My evening visits continued until 10:00 p.m. when she seemed to settle down. She slipped in to a comatose condition. I talked to her and sometimes I thought she could hear me.

Walt and Ian were kept apprised of her condition, and on January 6, 2000, the four of us were in Rhondda's room at the hospital. I went home that night at 9:30 p.m. to get some rest. The call came at 5:45 a.m. Rhondda had died quietly as a nurse was preparing to bathe her. After a moment's reflection, I called our sons. None of us were surprised. Ian rushed to join me at the hospital. Walt in Columbia took longer.

According to her wishes, Rhondda was cremated. A well-attended memorial service was conducted at First Presbyterian Church, a couple of blocks from the house, where we were members and I had been attending Sunday school. The service was led by Dr. Roger Gullick, who had come to the Florence pulpit from our Presbyterian church in Salisbury, and the eulogy was delivered by my friend, Bill Moran. I asked the boys if they wanted anything special in the service, and Walt asked the organist to play "Waltzing Matilda." The bush ballad and unofficial Australian national anthem brought smiles to the congregants. The service ended, and family and friends retreated to a dining room for a lunch prepared by the women of the church.

Three days later, our sons and I, along with Marvin Lynch, were standing in the Smith Family cemetery plot in Harriman to inter her ashes. Marvin directed the graveside service with my siblings and their spouses in attendance, except for Oba, and many of the nieces and nephews were present as well. The simple grave marker reads:

> Rhondda Miller-Smith
> Born in Brisbane, Australia
> 3-17-1920   1-7-2000

The family and friends gathered for lunch before we returned to South Carolina. I had been alone in the house for the past three years, so coming home to an empty house was nothing new. But my routine of going to the nursing home to spend eight or nine hours with Rhondda was now oddly at an end. I felt some guilt that I was here and she was not. I felt some remorse when using something around the house that was hers. For months, I would wake in the middle of the night and listen for her before remembering she was not there.

OLD AGE

Growing old has its lessons. By staying in Florence, I thought I would always have a pool of contemporaries with whom to socialize. The reality is much different. Not all my friends enjoyed good health. As I went deeper into my eighties, some were too frail to get out of the house, and many passed on to the other side. That fact was evident even last night (February 7, 2002) at a reception for a bank official at the South Carolina Country Club, not far from FMU. To my dismay and disappointment, I found no one even approximating my generation in age, and I saw very few familiar faces. Though it would be normal to consider moving into a retirement center at my age, I do not feel old enough. Socializing with people my own age is appealing, but age would be all we had in common. From my experience with Rhondda, Heritage, and Lowman, I have a fair assessment of what to expect of the other residents. Walt has said many times, "Dad, you're not ready for that." With Ian and Jeanie here in Florence, and sometimes Loren and Brewster, I have a reason to stay. That is not to say I have not considered a condo in South Florida for the cooler months and another in the mountains for the warmer ones. Inertia also comes with age, and I am reluctant to make the effort to travel. Were Rhondda still alive and well, I am sure we would have travelled the world often, but as my six weeks of solo visits to Japan, Korea, Taiwan, and Hong Kong taught me, it can be lonely knowing no one, always among strangers, dining alone, and having no one with whom to share the sights. I would not enjoy travelling without a companion.

I watched the 2002 Orange Bowl on January 2, turning off the Florida-versus-Maryland match at half-time and going to bed. I did not "have a dog in the fight," and the contest was of no consequence to me. In my old age, my interest in sporting events, movies, celebrity happenings and such pop-culture matters never achieved fan status, but has diminished further, solidly replaced by worry, which is an integral part of being a parent, further amplified by being a grandparent. I focus and perhaps sometimes fixate on the welfare of my son's and their families. How will they stand up to the challenges that are most certainly before them? I worry, perhaps unnecessarily, about Loren and Brewster. Will they succeed in life, be happy, and be content in their old age? I worry less about Miller and Hayden, only because of their ages, not yet immersed in adolescence, when parenting succumbs to the influences of society, but their time is coming. Will they make good decisions? The best I can do is remain relevant to them, talk and listen to them frequently. Be there for them. And then, I still worry.

While procreation is the primary mission of all species, producing a next generation that is improved over the last should be the enhanced mission of mankind. But we are so casual about it, uninformed and careless about it when child-rearing should take precedence over all other matters. Too often, kids hit the street at age thirteen, and only with luck survive to realize any part of their potential.

There are stages lived in reaching old age, and each brings its own perspective, shaped by the previous stages. The notion that the future stretches out before you is lost to the past. I wake up feeling good, generally optimistic, happy to be alive, and ready to enjoy another day. In the past, I have said that my outlook on life hasn't really changed much over the years. That is not entirely accurate. I am essentially the same person I was fifty years ago, but the positive outlook I had when I woke up this morning is the culmination of fine tuning, adjusting outlook for present age-induced reality. In advanced age, greater attention is given to the condition of the body and the gradual failings. Expectations for yourself change. The wisdom and experiences of the accumulated years can inform our appraisal of people, events, and ideas. Outlook changes, but I am still essentially the same guy I was fifty years ago.

Today, my "ten-year plan" has been abbreviated. I am still optimistic enough to schedule events for three months into the future. Beyond that, my RSVPs read "maybe."

EPILOGUE

In retirement, Dad returned to gardening and canning, and he never lost his taste for cornbread, which he combined with broccoli in the mix. His relationship with figs also continued, planting several of the fruit-bearing trees in his backyard, touching off his battle with the high-flying Wallenda's of the animal world, acrobatic squirrels that competed for the figs. Nets were thrown over the plants and contrived obstructions to their climbing were installed. New trees were planted away from the house, garage, and other trees from which the furry menaces could leap, and a single shot, air pump, Daisy BB gun was handy to the backdoor to deliver a discouraging sting. About one hundred jars of fig jelly littered the floor of the laundry room, a table and counter, which I am sure were destined to be gifts to his neighbors. He was generous like that. He would visit Ian and Jeanie in Ashville, returning to Florence with a trunk laden with apples that he would then distribute to neighbors and friends, which sometimes returned to him in the form of apple pies.

I found the picture of Dad and the crew of PT-138, mugging for the camera in Tacloban or Ormoc Bay, enlarged and framed it. On one of his visits, he picked up the frame and pointed to one of the sailors, identifying him a gunner's mate, Cosmo Treva. He lamented that the American cemetery at Aitape may have been washed away by a typhoon years ago. On Christmas Day of 2019, as I wrote about Dad's return from leave in Sydney, typhoon Phanfone struck Tacloban.

Dad's preparation for the hurricane that spared Tallahassee was informed by his experience in mid-December, 1944, at Tacloban Bay. Typhoon Cobra assaulted naval forces throughout the Philippine Sea with wind speeds clocked at 120 mph. From about 260 miles east-northeast of Tacloban, Task Force 38 had been conducting raids on Japanese airfields in the Philippines. In connection with that operation the United States Third Fleet, commanded by Admiral William "Bull" Halsey, had been conducting refueling operations. But as the weather worsened, and those operations had to be terminated. Perhaps acting upon inaccurate information about the location and direction of the typhoon, on December 17, Admiral Halsey unwittingly sailed the fleet into the center of the typhoon with cataclysmic consequences. In winds gusting to 160 mph, high seas, and torrential rain, three destroyers capsized and sank with 790 souls lost. Over one hundred aircraft were either wrecked or washed overboard from carriers and as many as twenty-seven other warships were damaged.

The storm came to be known as "Halsey's typhoon." A court of inquiry was conducted aboard the USS Cascade in the Caroline Islands, north of New Guinea. Admiral Nimitz was in attendance. In a divided vote, the court found that Halsey had committed an error in judgement but failed to conclude sanctioning was appropriate. In the following month, Halsey surrendered his command of the Third Fleet.

PT-138 was placed in service on September 29, 1942, armed with one 40 mm, one 37 mm, and two 20 mm mounted cannons, four twenty-one-inch torpedoes, and two twin .50-caliber machine guns. On October 24, 1945, while Dad was on assignment in Cuba, PT-138 was placed out of service, stripped and destroyed at Samar, Philippines, the area in which it had harassed the Japanese in service to our country. As he returned the four PTs from Cuba for decommissioning, he must have considered the fate of the boat on which he had spent the past year.

As Mom and Dad visited my home from time to time, I visited my parents in Florence. On one such occasion, Mom and I were sitting on a bench outside the backdoor of the Graham Street house.

Like Dad, I tried to get her out of the depressingly dark paneled room where she spent most of her days and into the sunlight. In a reconciled tone, she surprised me with, "I'm becoming my mother." I knew she was right and made no reply. In that moment, she was aware of her condition at Lowman, where again, we sat on a bench, taking in the sunshine, and I worked at engaging her in conversation, talking about Miller and Hayden. My son was quite young, but the concern Hayden had about Nana in her wheelchair stays with me. I thought it might be entertaining and somewhat therapeutic if I brought the kids out to visit her. "I don't want them to remember me this way," she replied to the suggestion. She was probably correct as my memory of my nana in a Florence nursing home has outlasted all others. Reading Dad's story, I think the Alzheimer years were more vexing for Dad than I fully understood at the time.

There was no hyperbole in Dad's description of his wife's wanderlust. In her youth, the Miller family followed "Pop" (Henry Miller) to India, where he worked his engineering magic to construct a pari-mutuel betting "tote board" at a horse-racing track. Before the war, Mom served as an airline stewardess for Australian National Airways, taking her on routes between the country's larger cities— plus Tasmania, New Zealand, and the Philippines. It was as glamorous a job as a woman in that time might imagine. Anything was better than a life standing still. But the airline had a dismal flight safety record, twelve crashes in twelve years between 1938 and 1950, including one off of Tacloban, where PT-138 would later be assigned. Disturbingly, several of those incidents were caused by simply running out of gas.

The grave marker Dad describes made its way to my cousin Jack's house in Birmingham, Alabama, Mom's traveling days did not end on January 7, 2000. Three days after the memorial service, we took her cremated remains to the family plot on the hill in Harriman, Tennessee, where Sybil and Wilma were laid to rest eighty-two years earlier, followed by other family members in the ensuing years. As the years passed, Dad grew disappointed with the "perpetual care" he was promised, but I think he did not like having her 385 miles away and that he wanted to be buried with her, but not there. As Jack later relayed to me in a phone call, Dad told his younger brother Wallace that he was moving her to the national cemetery in Florence. With nothing more said, Wallace then took it upon himself to return to the cemetery on the hill, where he pulled her boxed remains from the soil and put in the trunk of his car, leaving the headstone behind. For a couple of weeks, she was a passenger in the back of Wallace's car before Dad could make the arrangements with the Florence National Cemetery for her reinterment there. I think years passed before Aunt Glenna instructed her son, Jack, to retrieve the headstone, and that is when I got his call. I promised I would pick it up if I ever passed through Birmingham again. It's not the kind of thing you leave on the street for pickup, but I wasn't sure what I would do with it. At least symbolically, Mom's traveling days were still not at an end.

As the television news was dominated by the memorial services for Queen Elizabeth II at St. Giles' Cathedral in Edinburgh, I found a text message from Jack attaching a video. It was a panoramic view of the countryside of Colorado surrounding his new house there outside of Buena Vista, a town of two-story storefronts on Main Street, surrounded by snow-capped mountains, where days end with blazing sunsets. As he panned through the Aspen trees, he lowered the lens to focus on Mom's Harriman headstone, the latest resident of Buena Vista, for now.

In the corner of my bedroom is a leather suitcase with my dad's navy uniform and campaign ribbons. I found it standing on end in the dark recesses of a closet in the paneled den of his house in Florence. I'm not sure what I will do with that either.

In my research for this book, I reviewed the photo albums that Mom had prepared for my brother and me. There are pages of pictures with her on dates with officers from several branches of the military and several countries. I am assuming those were also arranged dates by Liz and other United Service Organizations (USO) volunteers. There are also newspaper clippings of her teaching semaphore and Morse code to naval officers. Quite attractive, she had clearly captured their full attention. She once described World War II as a "romp." I guess for her it was.

The recollection my father had for names, places, and events from sixty years ago is striking, when I can't remember what I had for breakfast. No less striking are the people whose paths he crossed. People we can "google" today and find, and others he met on his journey through college, the war, and beyond. He recalls guys who trained with him at the midshipman's school at Columbia University and finding them a year later at Times Square. There was the navy nurse he met in Newport, finding her again in New Hebrides, where he unceremoniously and comically splashed into the water with her. He was coached by Ann Elizabeth Curtis, an Olympic swimmer. President Kennedy, only seventy miles from his family home in Hyannisport, may have been at the party with Commander John D. Bulkeley. Boston Chief of Police Ed McNamara may still have his Colt .45 pistol.

Until I undertook editing the manuscript, I knew more about the war and the role of PT boats in the South Pacific from episodes of *McHale's Navy* than I learned from Dad. Until I read in the manuscript about the party for Commodore Harlee, I thought the "torpedo juice" mentioned in many episodes was of the home-distilled variety, but it was real. In fact, I may have a bottle taken from Dad's sparse liquor cabinet while cleaning out the house. Mom shared some of what he shared with her, but it wasn't much and very little of it appeared in the manuscript, which is striking in its detail and specific in its recollection of names, places, and events.

Dad's drive through the tropical jungle of Samar to remote Guiuan was rewarded by finding the Immaculate Conception Catholic Parish Church built in a Baroque architectural style in 1718, 227 years before my father passed through its threshold. Sadly, the church was demolished by Typhoon Haiyan in 2013, and restoration efforts have been ongoing since.

Dad speculated that the navy cannon turret installed over the portico to the NROTC building was still there. Finding the Michigan NROTC Facebook page, I sent an inquiring message that was favored with a reply. A new building was constructed and neither the cannon turret nor the building are still there.

I don't know why he stopped writing when he did. He made more memories after November 22, 2004, when he signed and dated the manuscript he simply called *My Life*. He continued to drive his 2000 Mercury Grand Marquis until late 2017, coming over for Hayden's baseball games or just to visit. For his first grandchild, Loren, Dad went online to be ordained by American Marriage Ministries in order to officiate and preside over the August 20, 2016 wedding of Loren and Cory Carlson at a bed-and-breakfast in Asheville. I don't think it was long after Dad signed off on the manuscript that he returned for a third time to Australia, this time with Ian's son, Brewster. He was an excellent traveling companion for Dad, who proudly told the story of meeting up with a group of senior travelers at the airport luggage carousel in Sydney. They were struggling to pull their bags off of the conveyor. Brew climbed up onto the carousel and began unloading the luggage identified by the grateful passengers.

Brewster later met Shaina Eckhouse, a Texas girl in Charleston pursuing her medical education which at some point deep into their relationship required her participation in a program in Florence. Briefly, she took up residence with Dad, who became so impressed with Shaina; he offered Brewster some relationship advice, "You need to put that girl under contract." They were soon engaged, and Reverend Smith was again expected to preside over a wedding, this time on the beach at the Isle of Palms; but by that time, Dad had answered his last calling.

It was a recent NCAA National Baseball Championship winning team that South Carolina head coach, Ray Tanner, brought to Florence on April 11, 2012. They were there to christen the new Cormell Field at Sparrow Stadium on the campus of Francis Marion, an NCAA Division II school with a solid record. Putting up a three-run third inning and a two-run seventh inning, FMU defeated the Gamecocks by a 5 to 4 margin, and Dad was there to see the historic win and called to tell me about it. It was around this same time that billboards promoting the heritage of Francis Marion University appeared around town bearing the image of my father and providing good material for kindly jabs from friends.

It was on March 1, 2014 that Ian and I unveiled the statue of Dad in the company of family from across the southeast, friends, and colleagues. Dad's home became a flop house for my cousins on every bed and couch. The statue was erected under a rotunda behind Stokes Hall, outside the door from which he had emerged in his commencement gown on his way to graduation exercises. The artist, Alex Palkovich, describes the event on his website (alexpalkovich.com) like this: "On the sun-kissed cool and breezy afternoon of March 1, the sons of FMU's first president, Dr. Doug Smith, unveiled a six-foot-two-inch bronze sculpture of the man who began its forty-three years of history." I am reminded of the opportunity my father recognized when we left Salisbury, to be the founding president of a college. He might have considered this a more fitting place to stop writing his story.

It was a life journey through one hundred years of personal and American history, from post "Great War" and the Spanish Flu in 1918 Harriman, through eighteen presidents, several wars, a Great Depression and a Great Recession, and seven colleges and universities, collecting friends and colleagues, and the memories he shares here. There was so much I did not know about him. Leading up to his introduction at the Governor's School awards dinner, I was called by the board member making the introduction, briefly interviewed and asked what one word describes my father. My answer was "duty." I could have replied with "humility, responsibility, integrity, service, or leadership"—all affirmative character traits that he exemplified, but "duty" implies an obligation. Living a moral life, the exercise of duty is what one expects of himself.

—Walt Smith

ABOUT THE AUTHOR

Walt Smith has been affiliated with a college or university for most of his life as the son of a professor and later college-founding president, and as an undergraduate and graduate student. Living in seven different college towns throughout the southeast, he graduated from the University of Alabama (BA), the University of South Carolina School of Law (JD), and most recently, the USC Linguistics Program (TESOL). A resident of Columbia, South Carolina, Walt is the son of Walter Douglas Smith and Rhondda Miller Smith, the brother of Ian Smith, the father of Miller and Hayden, and grandfather of Rhys and Luna. This book was written to honor his father's life of service to his country, family, students, and community.

CPSIA information can be obtained
at www.ICGtesting.com
Printed in the USA
BVHW081217160223
658645BV00001B/182